Crossing

Crossing

Sal Taylor Kydd

Down East Books
Published by Down East Books
An imprint of Globe Pequot Publishing Group, Inc.
64 South Main Street
Essex, CT 06426
www.globepequot.com
www.downeastbooks.com

Distributed by NATIONAL BOOK NETWORK

British Library Cataloguing in Publication Information available

Library of Congress Cataloging-in-Publication Data available
ISBN 9781684751969 (cloth)
ISBN 9781684751976 (ebook)

∞™ The paper used in this publication meets the minimum requirements of American National Standard for Information Sciences—Permanence of Paper for Printed Library Materials, ANSI/NISO Z39.48-1992.

For Simon

Introduction

Elin Spring

What is life, but a crossing? We are ever crossing. Amidst the perpetual rhythms of earth and sea, we embark upon passages charted since antiquity and borne by serendipity. In this volume of images and poetry, Sal Taylor Kydd bridges her own family's recurrent crossing to ancestral islands and invites us to share the journey.

Her crossings trace time, image by image and phrase by phrase. They coax memories embedded in stoic coastlines, forests and fields and in the traces left by those gone before. Sepia-tinted contemporary photographs are interwoven with poetry anchoring voices from past voyages. With reverence and optimism, Taylor Kydd grasps that life has always been indelibly shaped by earthly forces. They reign like sentinels testifying to our brief mooring here.

In a refined blend of figurative and gestural expression, Taylor Kydd's photographs are resolutely spare and jewel-like, their warm, rich tonalities enveloping us in an intimate embrace. They alight on the stillness between storms. Each scenario reveals a genial symbiosis between natural surroundings and the structures that natives and settlers built from them. In one image, a fencepost supports a tangle of climbing vines, while on the adjoining page an arched tree branch hosts a tire swing. Weathered buildings taunt a precarious balance of power. Beached vessels reiterate the flow of generations as continuous as the tides. Inherited belongings wistfully attest to the emotional solace that starchy traditions must have offered ancestors arriving to harsh new frontiers. In her tranquil, isolated spaces, Taylor Kydd offers a reprieve from taciturn seas, a space for reflection.

Her metaphoric crossings are buoyed by compositions with discrete visual elements in striking counterpoint to placid backdrops that invoke safe harbors. Fog mutes sound and obscures destinations, holding us in the present moment. Lens-based selective focus and subtle vignetting abet the hushed eloquence of Taylor Kydd's deceptively simple compositions. Blurry, wind-blown branches or shadows cast by the sinking sun underscore fleeting time. Like a breath of fresh salt air, a luminous lake or shimmering seascape inspire both vast perspectives and introspection.

In one photograph, a young child and an antique clipper ship ponder opposite horizons. Whether a sole passenger or an assembly of sailors, from generations ancient or modern, Taylor Kydd proffers that we all make our crossing on the same seas.

Foreword

Kat Kiernan

My memories of Maine's Penobscot Bay islands are distorted by time. I remember them not by name (Monhegan, Vinal Haven, Deer, Matinicus, Eagle, North Haven) but by experience: the beach with the good sea glass, the harbor where we slipped an anchor, a Labor Day weekend fogged in. Sal Taylor Kydd photographs blurred vignettes through slivers of selective focus. The distortion is like searching for shore after surfacing from a swim, saltwater still stinging the eyes. Although it has been years since I lived on the coast of Maine, her photographs stir a longing for tall pine trees and cold saltwater.

Beginning with the sea crossing, we follow her voyage in chapters punctuated with her poetry. Leaving the mainland behind, there is a shift in the air as temperatures cool and winds pick up. Island life is hard. Salt permeates everything, corroding pipes and warping floorboards. Long periods of difficult at times treacherous weather can make for an isolating existence. But Kydd's photographs are not stark or bleak, instead they embrace this solitude without evoking feelings of loneliness. They reflect a past that weighs heavily on the land.

The islands are shaped by the generations that built them. They hold stories of the Penobscot people who named them, and the fishing communities that followed. Dirt paths forged by footsteps lead to weathered, shingled homes. She finds connections with these surroundings, rendering their atmosphere and secrets. Attuned to the rhythms of island life, Kydd elegantly connects the natural and the manmade. She gives us a photograph of billowing laundry drying in the yard and pairs it with a gull riding the same air current.

Although similar in size and topography, each island has its own unique culture. One can travel between them by boat, mail plane, or public ferry, venturing further and further into the Atlantic.

I have sailed to Matinicus many times. It sits 20 miles off the Maine coast the most remote island on the Atlantic seaboard. Meaning "Far Out Island" in Abenaki, on a calm day one feels as though they might sail off the edge of the earth. Kydd wanders its two-mile length with quiet anticipation. Home to fewer than 100 year-round residents, Matinicus is a world all its own.

Despite the isolation, bonds are tightest within these island communities. She writes of the cemetery on Vinalhaven and the family names that dominate the stones. In one photograph of a gravestone inscribed "Still in Love" we understand that this place is so much a part of its people that eventually they become a part of it, too, still in love.

Island time moves slowly, but it does not stand still. Today, islander populations have dwindled some to as low as the single digits. But the land, structures, and objects hold memories. Kydd photographs these simple objects with reverence. Each one contains a story of a life lived on beloved land. Even the fog is laced with history, filtering the light to illuminate an anchor hauled out of the sea, resting on the lawn as a symbol of refuge. Kydd makes space for the past, allowing it to speak through her photographs.

this is the land of porcelain, lace, and old silver glinting

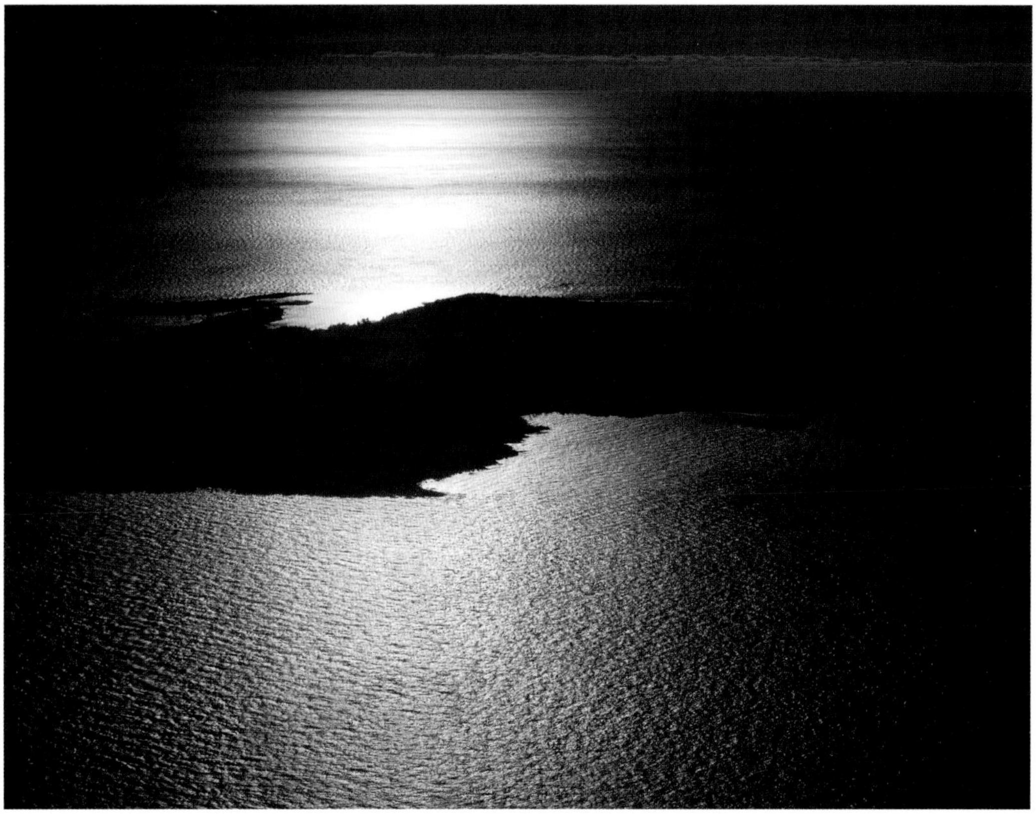

Crossing

We hug our arms against our chests,
and flap like chilly birds,
to warm and brace ourselves
against the stinging wind
that snaps unkindly
at our faces.

The ferry groans and shifts.
Like an old lady,
she makes her way
across the bay,
begrudging and proud
altogether.

Huddled on benches,
we squint at the cold.
Like hardy parishioners,
embattled and hopeful,
we soldier on,
still tethered
by this crossing
of the sea.

Across the bay
the island sleeps,
waiting out
the hard embrace
of winter.

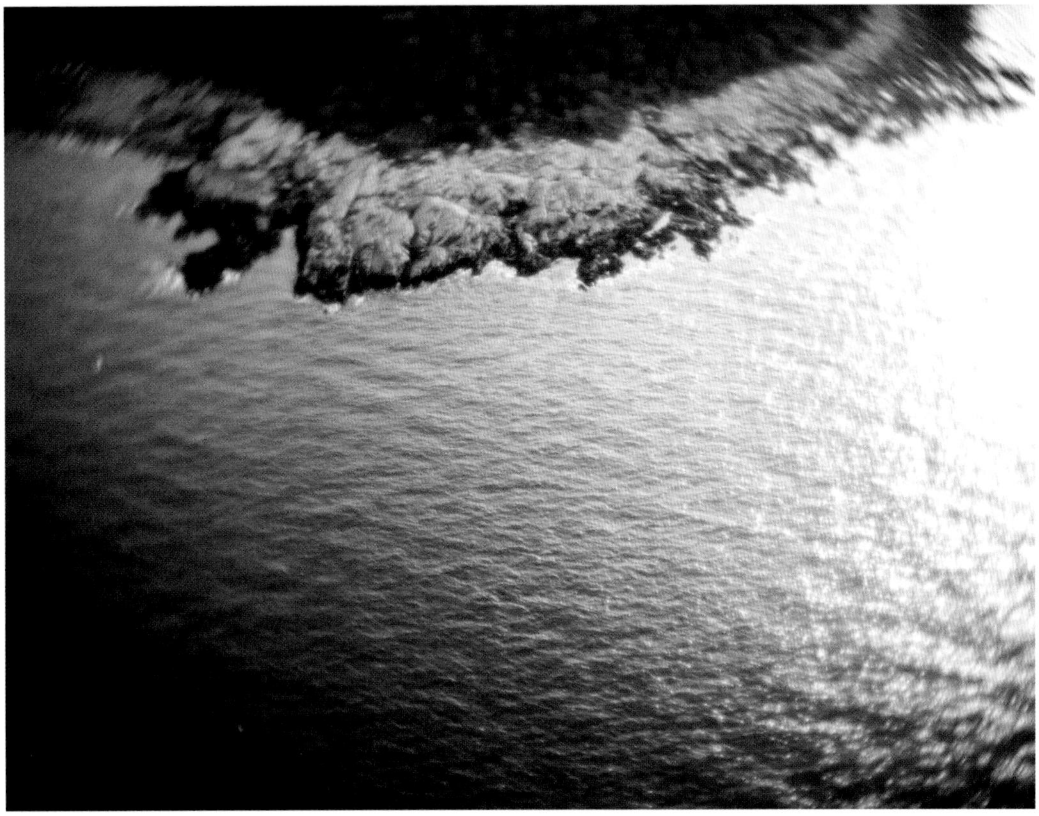

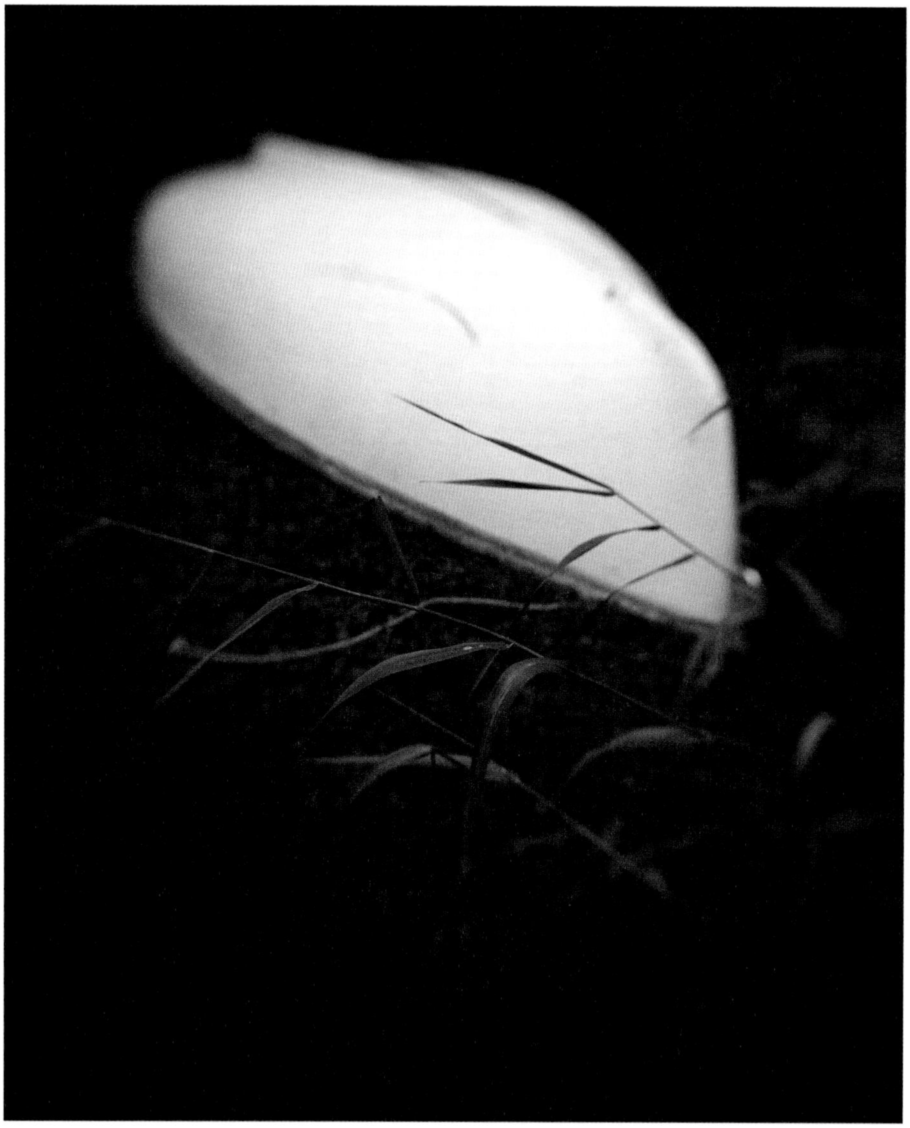

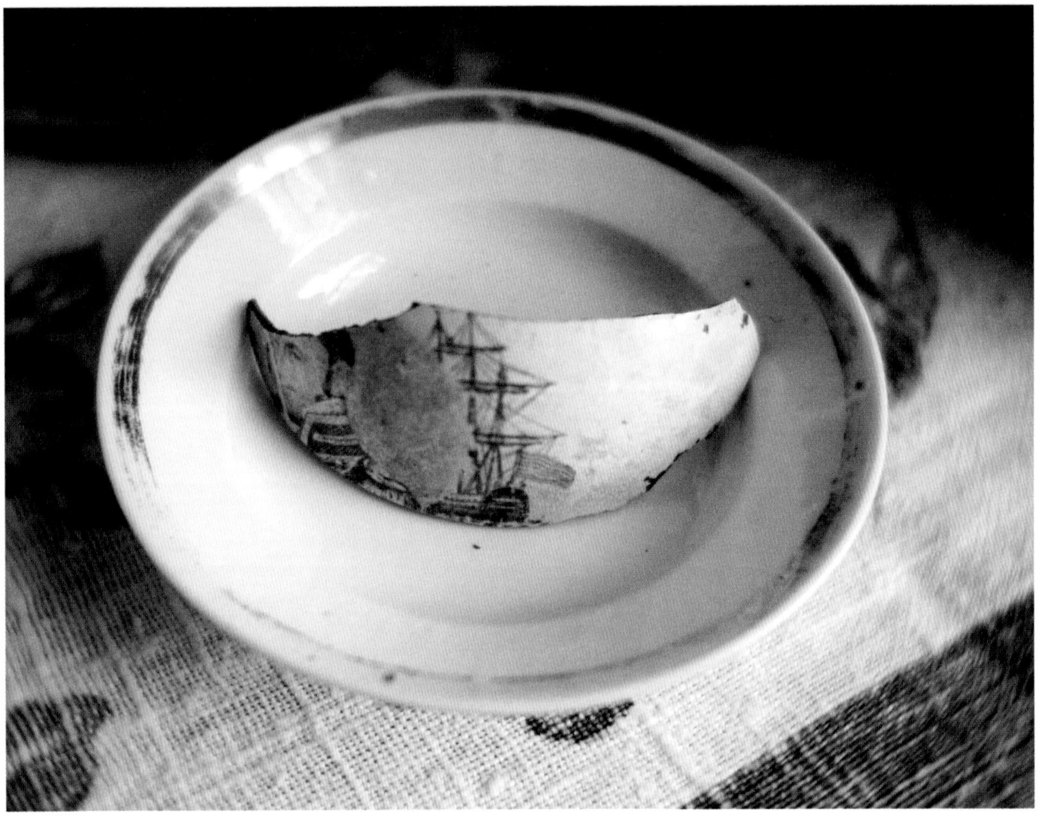

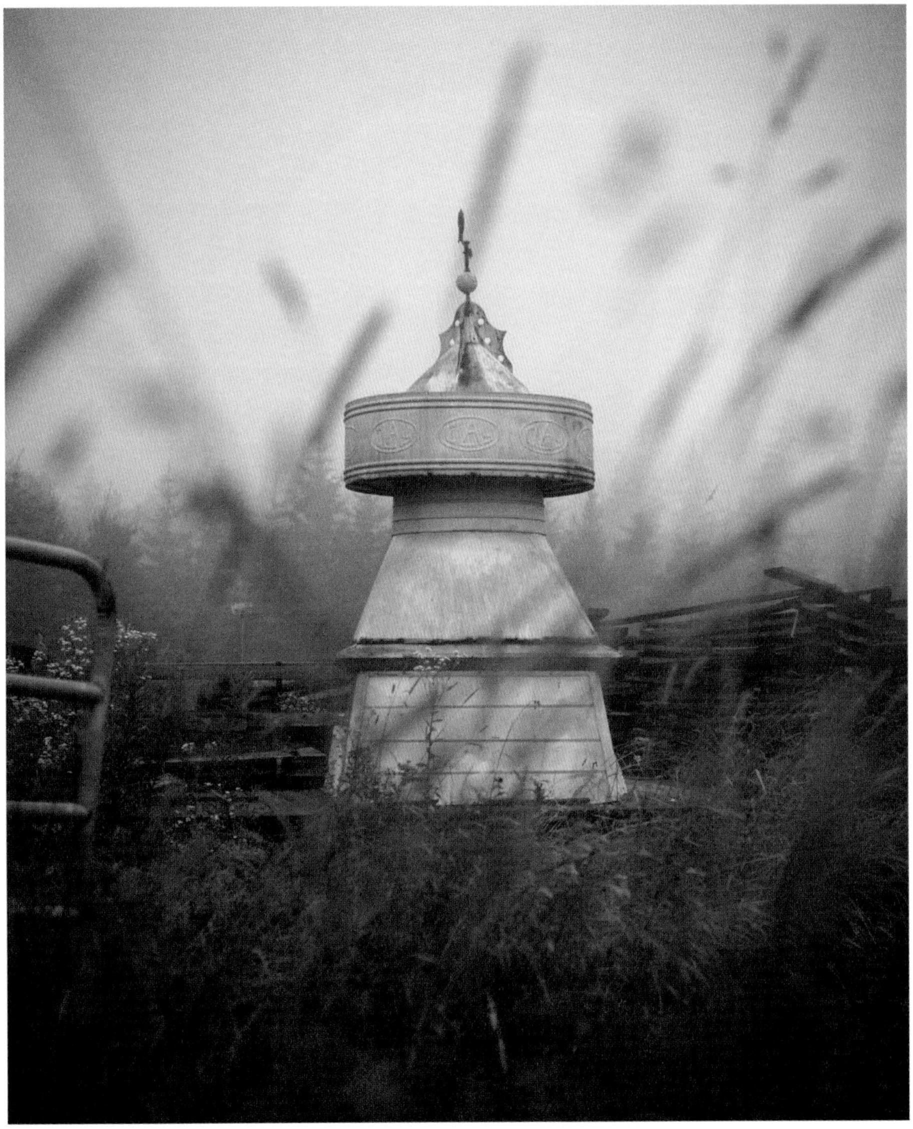

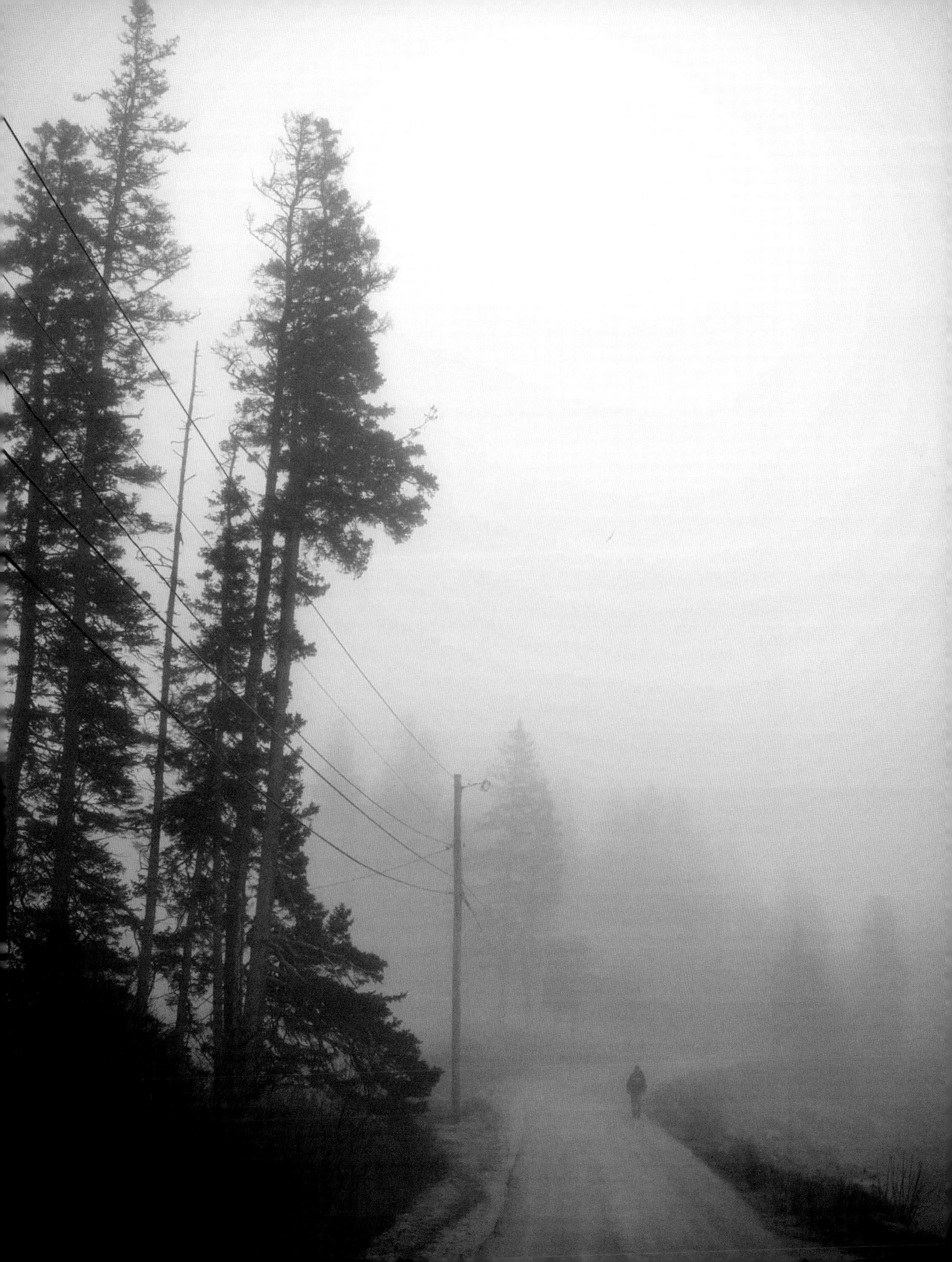

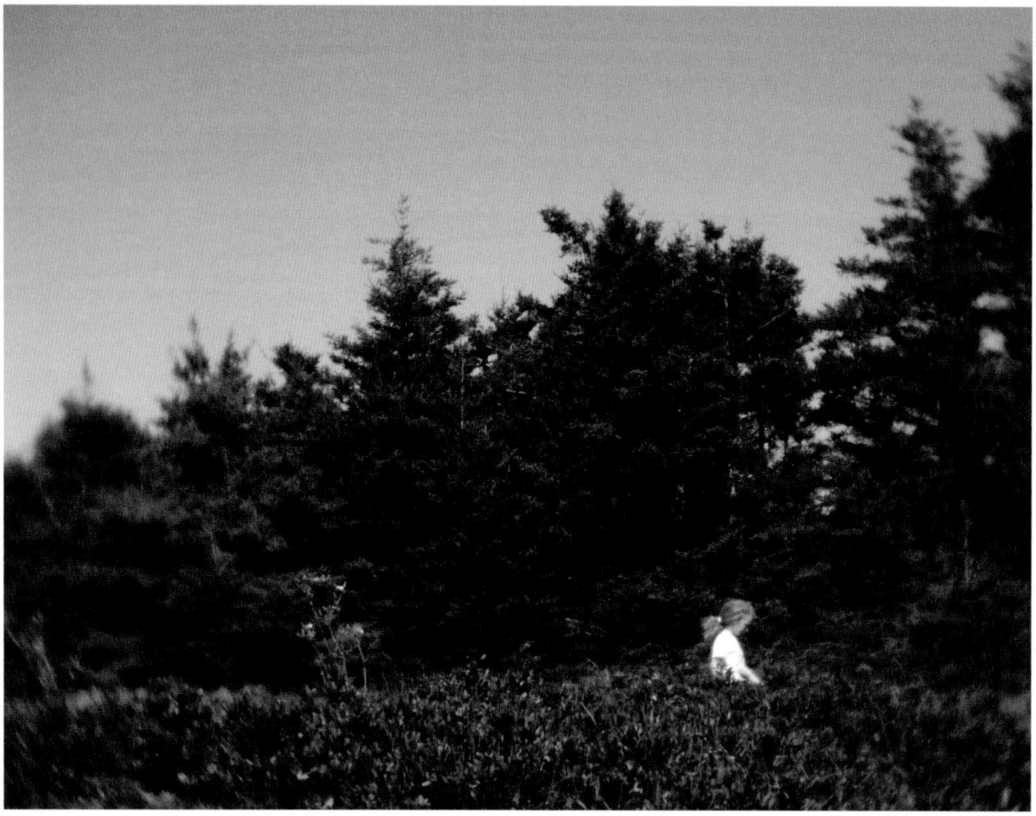

Onward

Uncertainly, I tread
the grassy path
that carves its way
through weathered turf,
and cleaves this land in two.

I pick my way through rocky knolls,
where outcroppings, like vertebrae
lead me through the island mist
along its verdant spine.

At one end lies a small dock,
its fragile tailbone perching
over roiling seas.
Summer homes, now shuttered
stand bereft, abiding.

At the school house
that stands vacant,
I stop and listen.
There, beneath the sound
of surf and birdsong,
I hear their distant voices.

I hear the chattering,
the small shoes scuffling,
chalk squealing,
and then, just as quickly
only the silent spring.

Onward to the well,
a lonesome bucket lies
discarded.
The path meanders, peters,
giving pause and asking,
whereto?

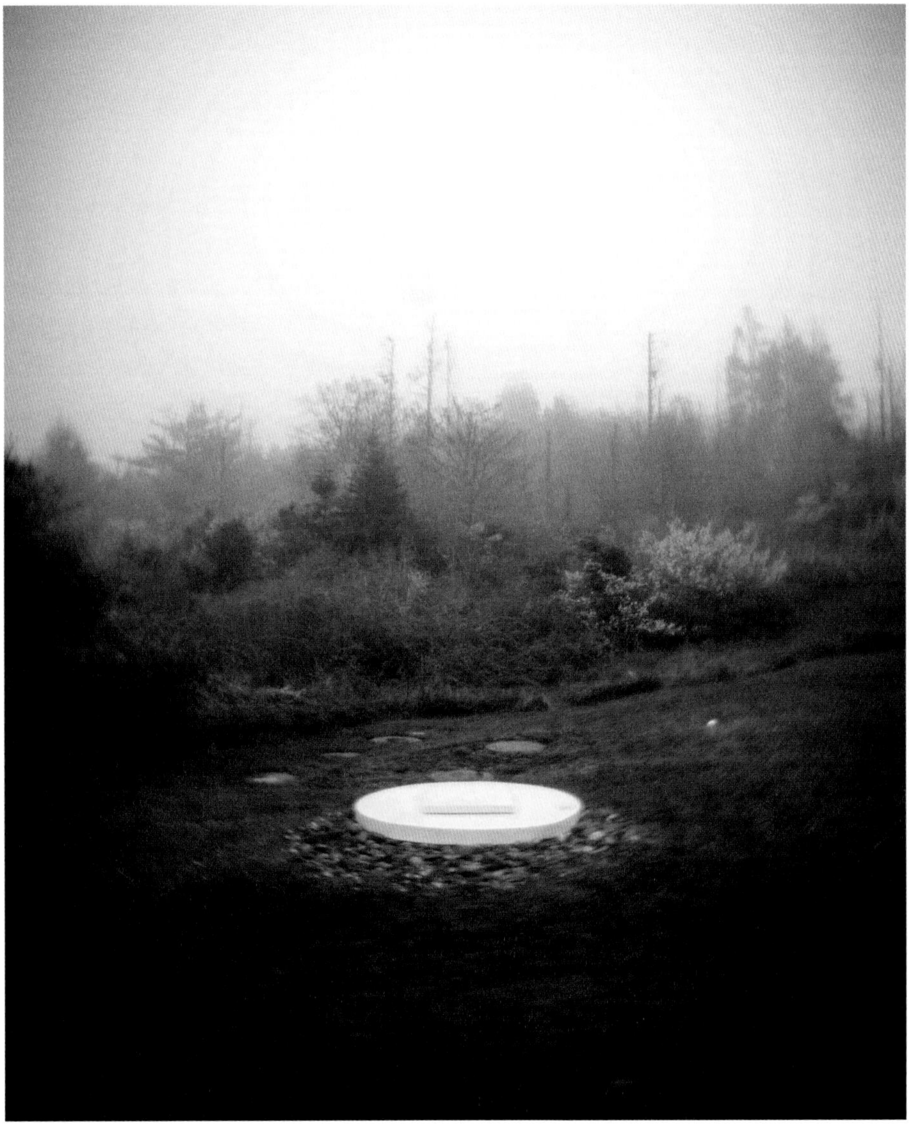

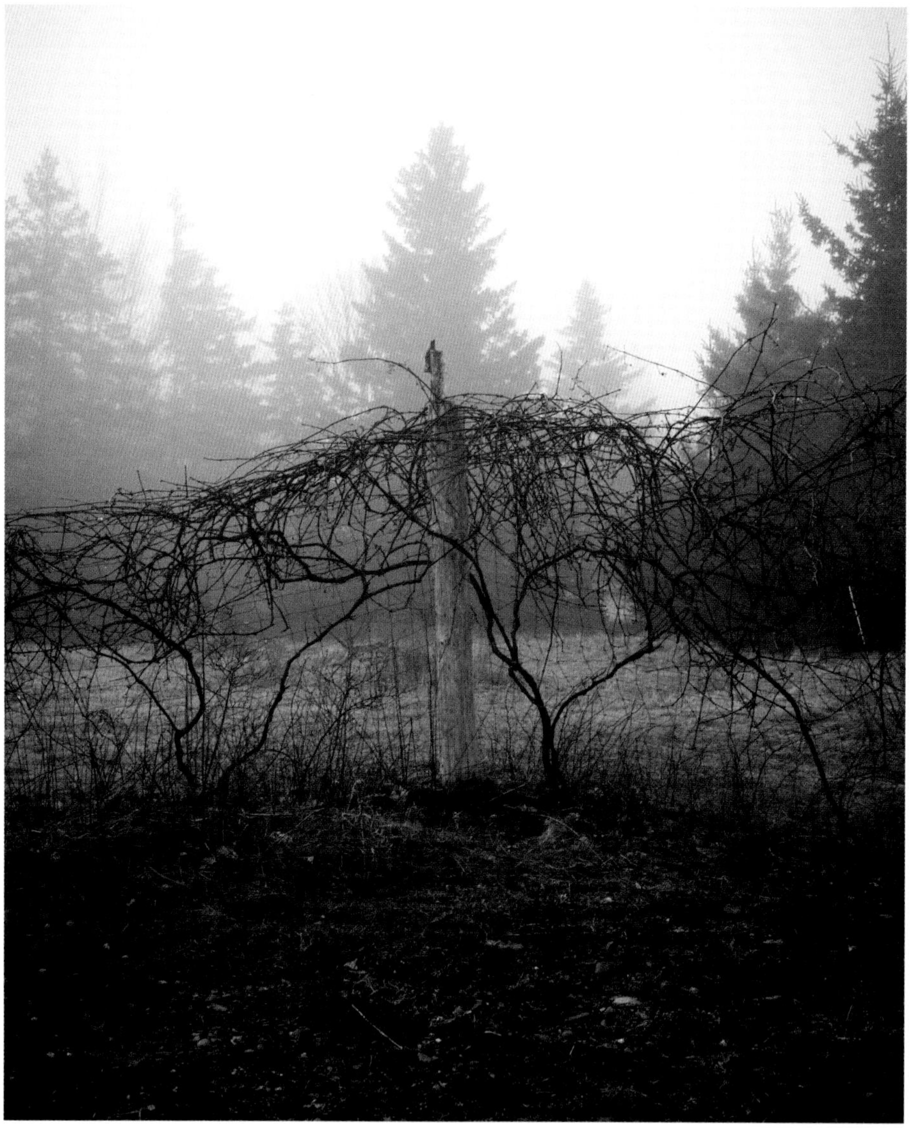

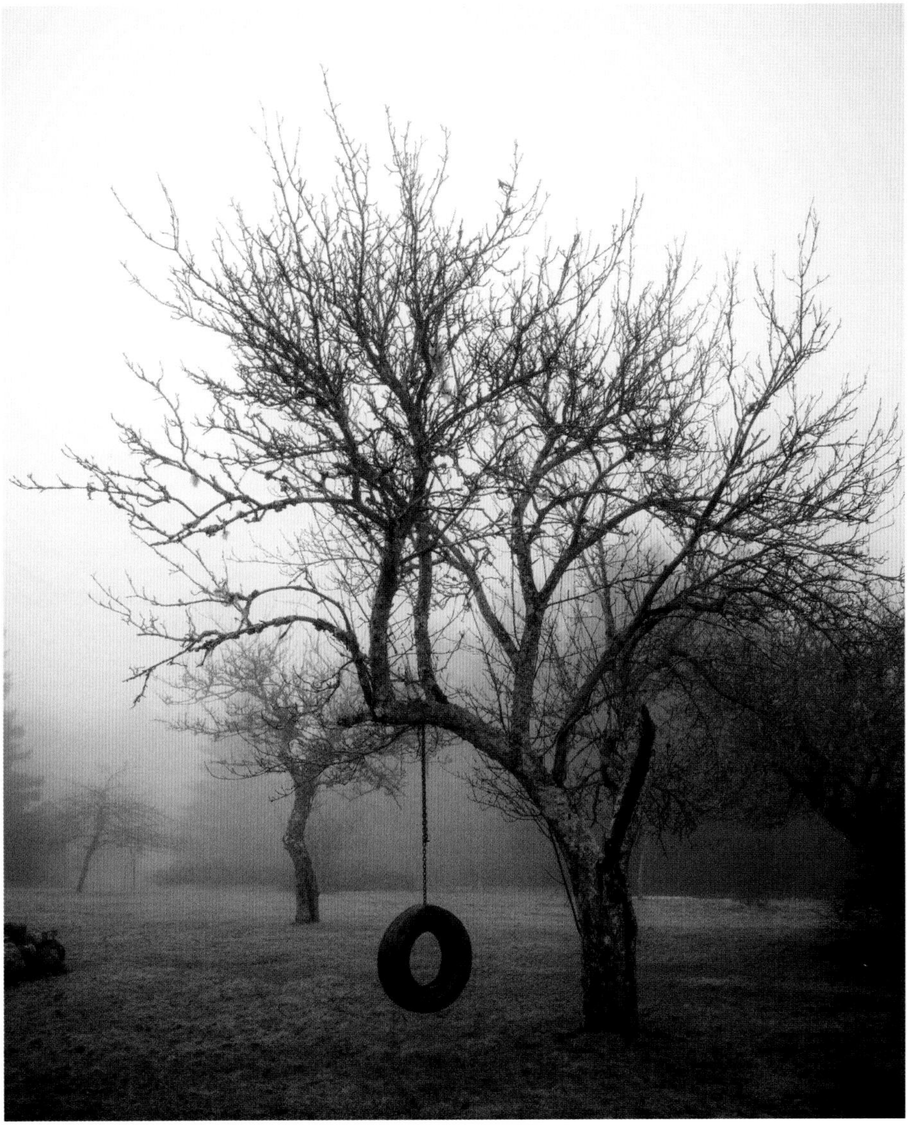

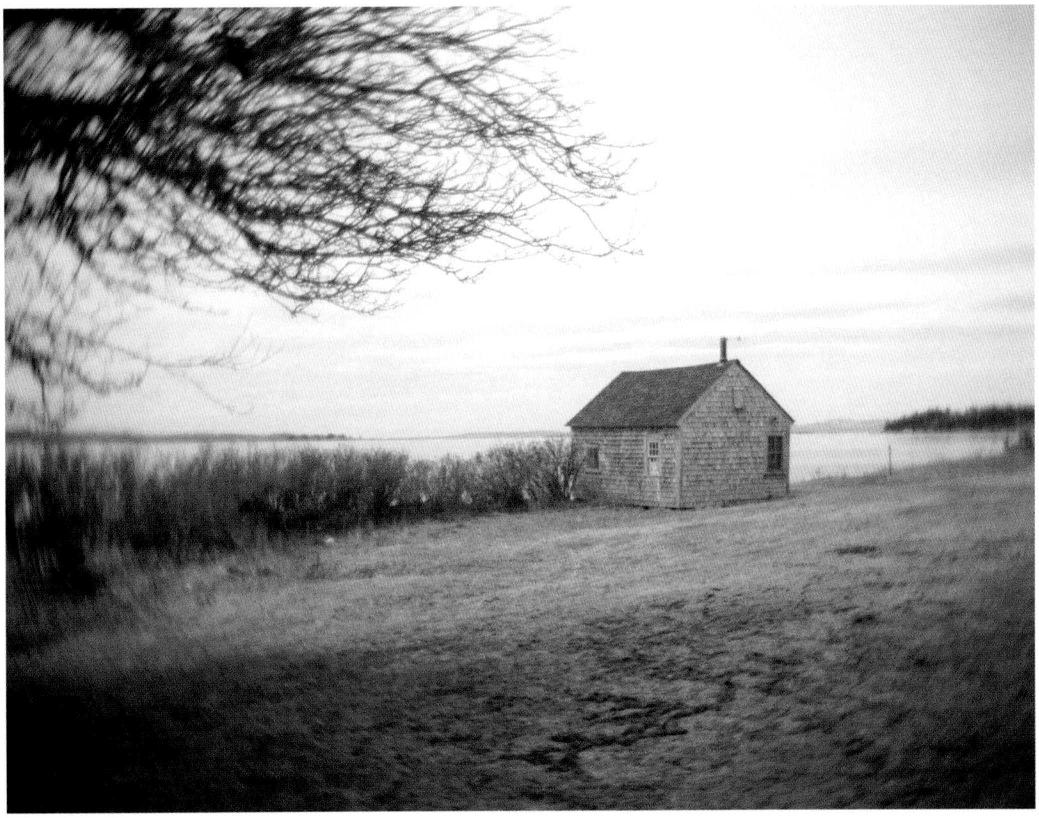

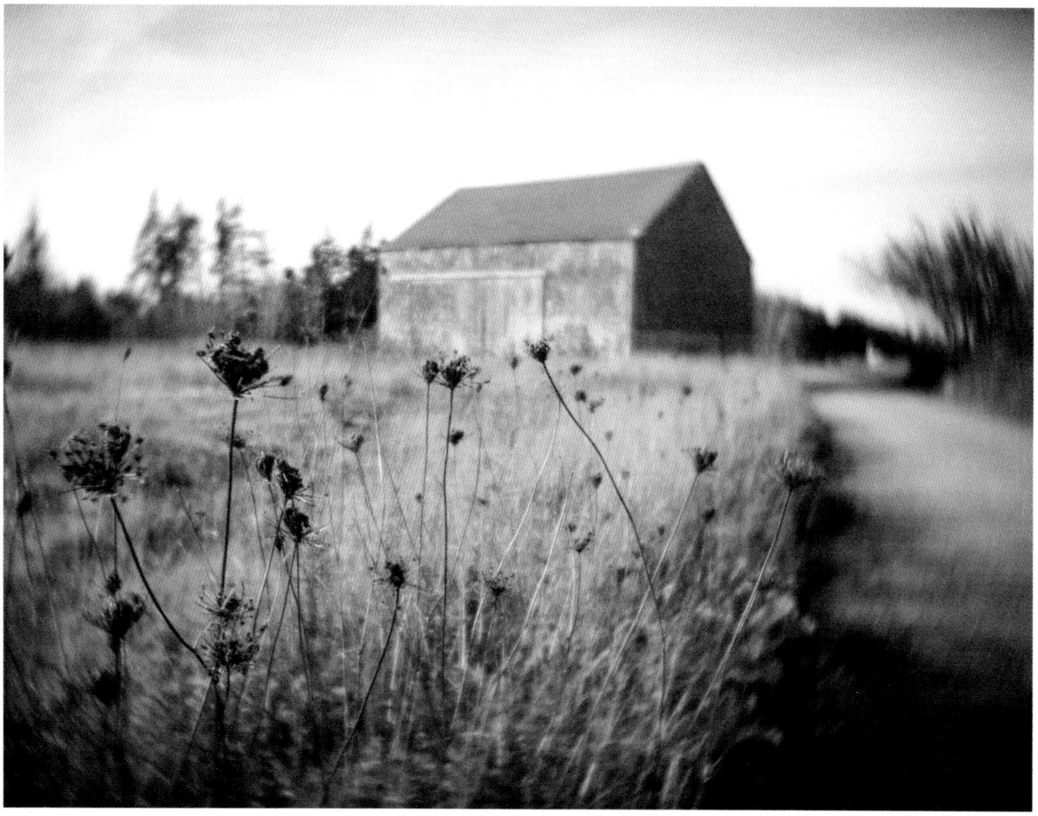

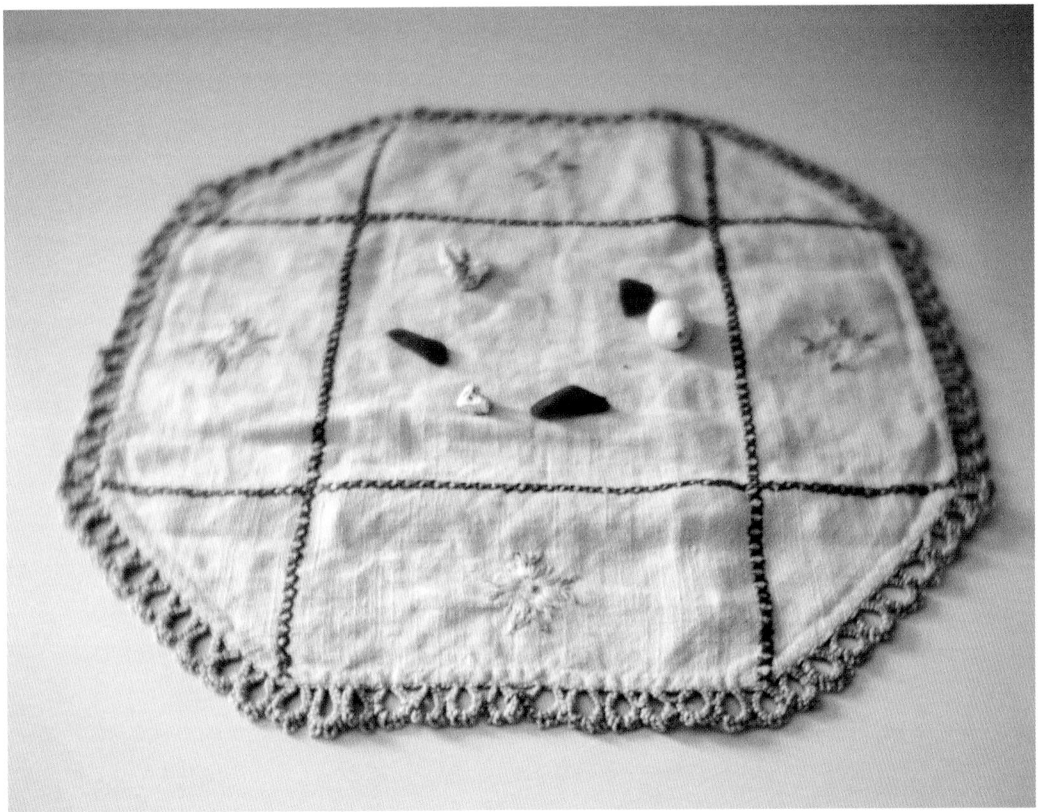

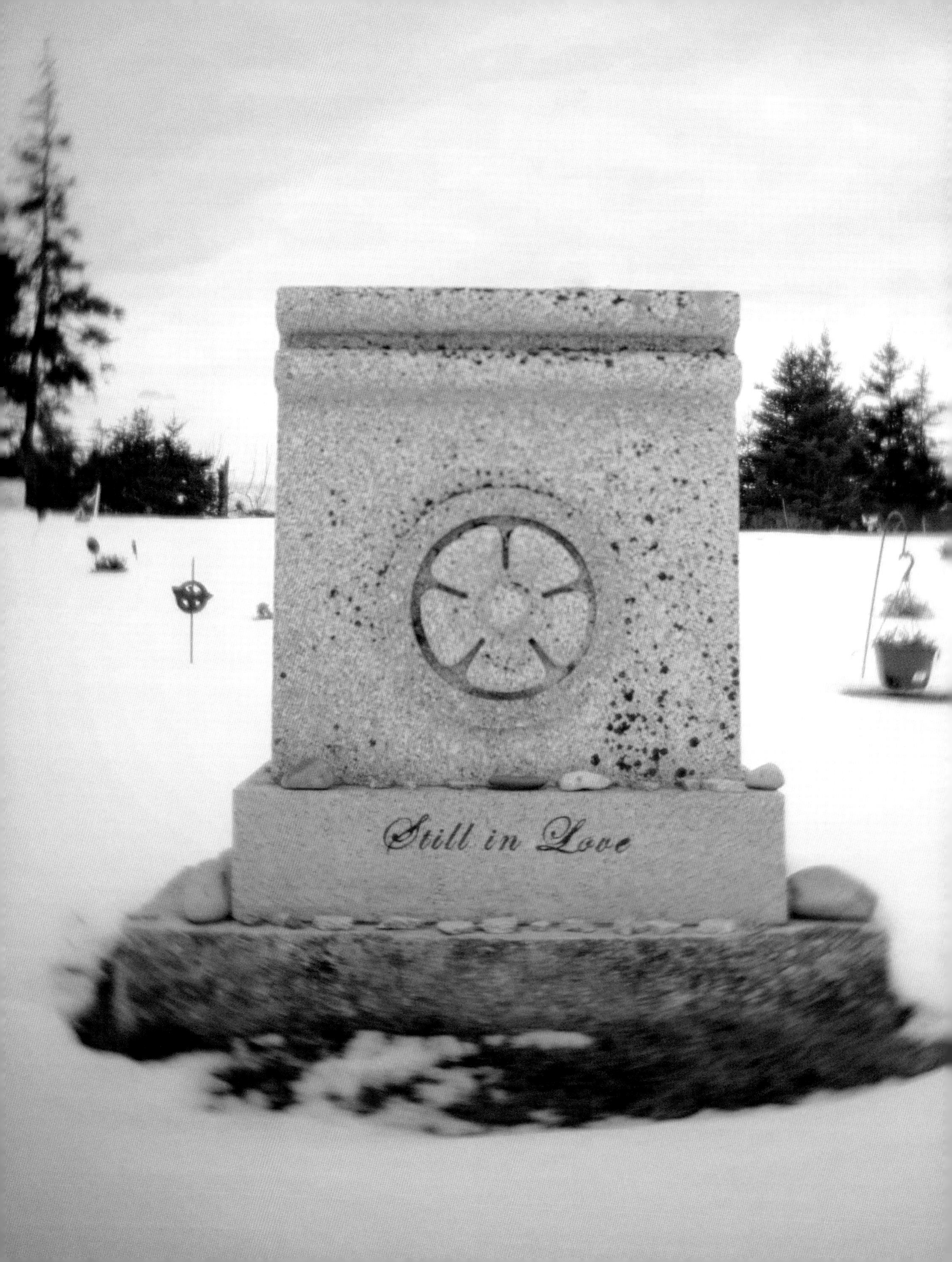
Still in Love

Vestige

It is November and the day is hard and shiny.
Winter sun lies low,
a bewitching light,
casting off the headlands.
Small planes glide in, buzzing,
landing softly.
Just shy of the drop
that awaits those who are
less careful.

Stillness settles.

In the cemetery, beneath the lichen,
lie the Youngs, Ames, Ridleys.
Bonds forged through
necessity and love,
retain the salty vestiges
of older claims pulled deeper.

Island history is hard won.
Objects telling stories of
repurposed usefulness,
are cherished by chapped hands
of generations past explaining.
Elders like old books kept close;
the air and salt embed their skin
with brittle melancholy.

This is the land of porcelain, lace
and old silver glinting.
Where apple trees, like old teachers,
stoop to proffer wisdom,
telling me of time's
relentless passing;
reminding me
of who was loved
and who stood bravely on.
Wind sweeping,
skirts flapping -
our own indomitable
ancestral kin.

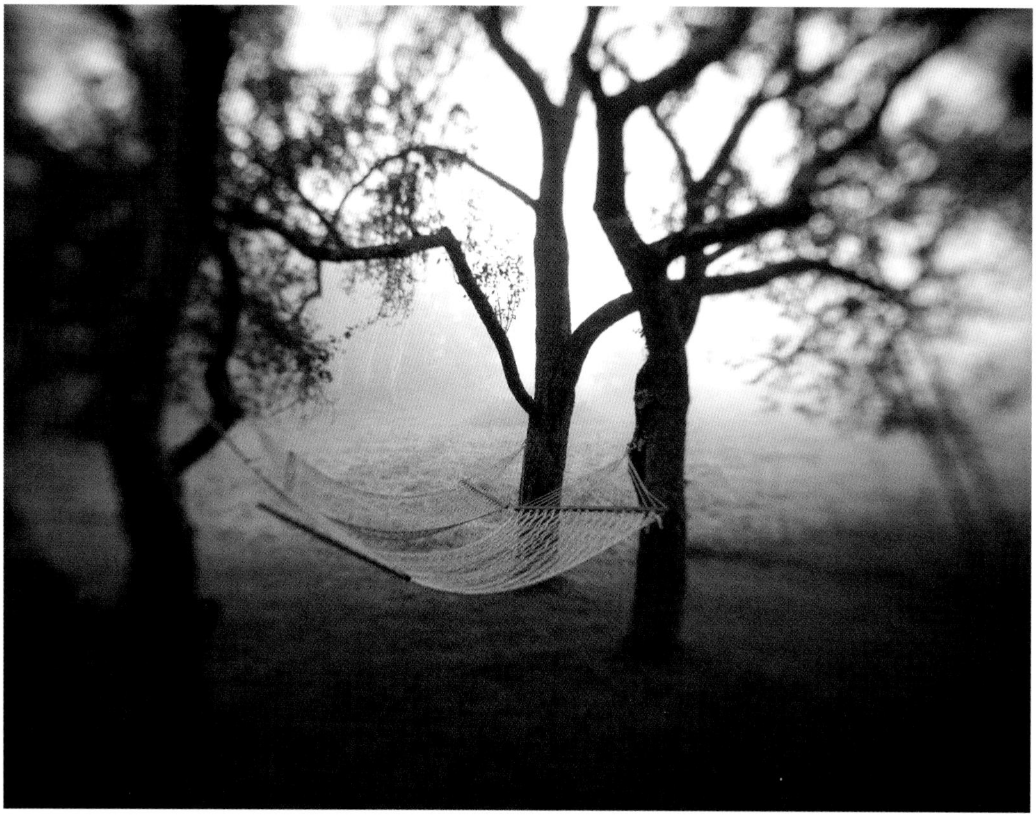

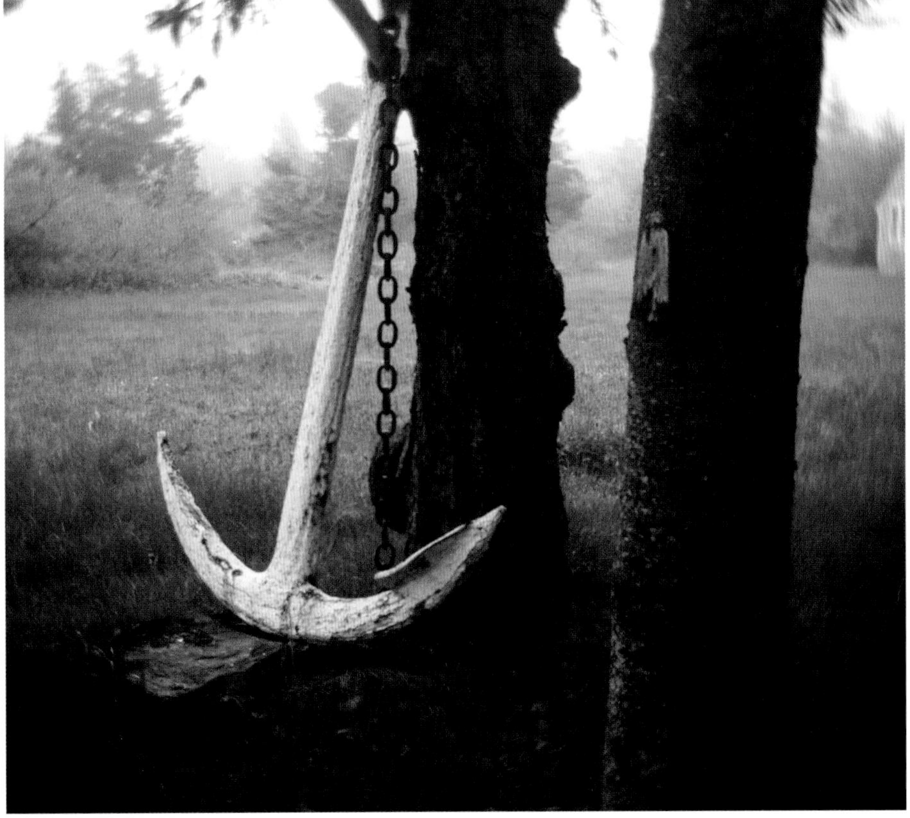

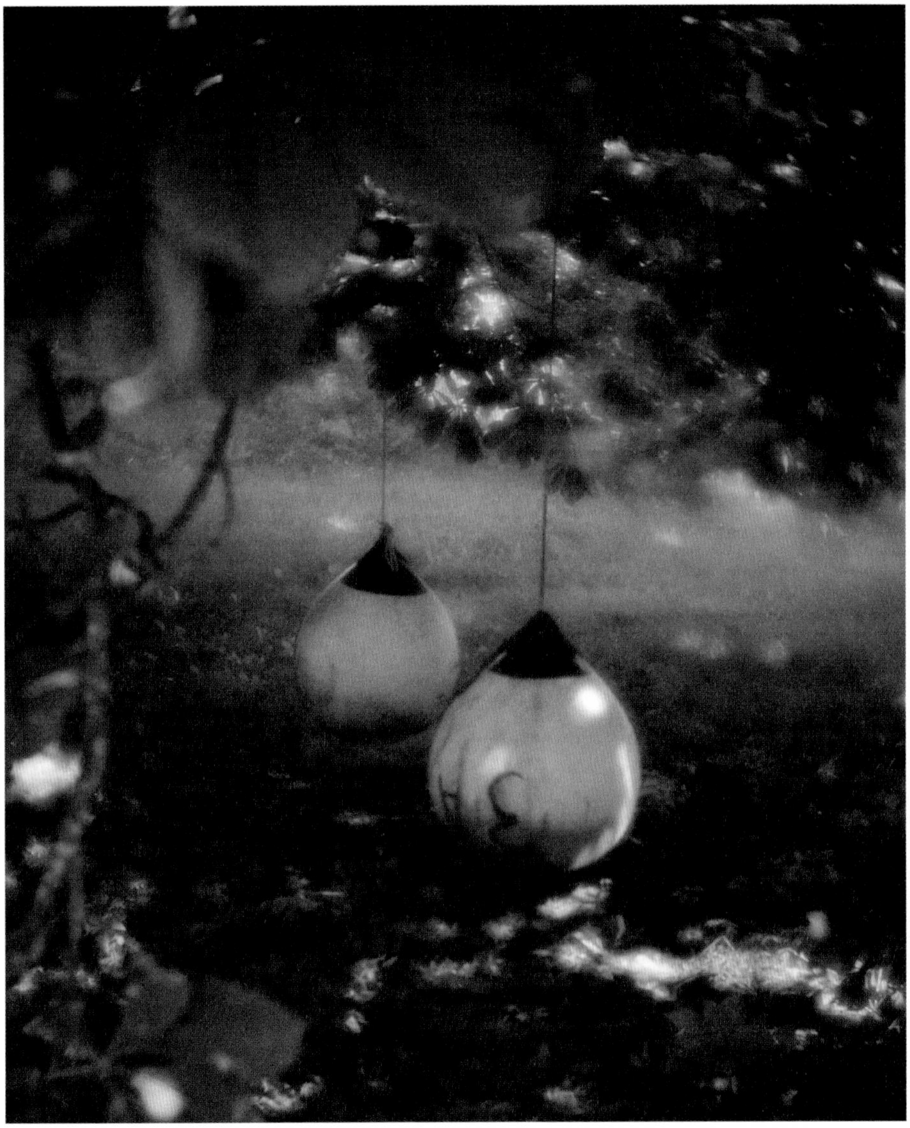

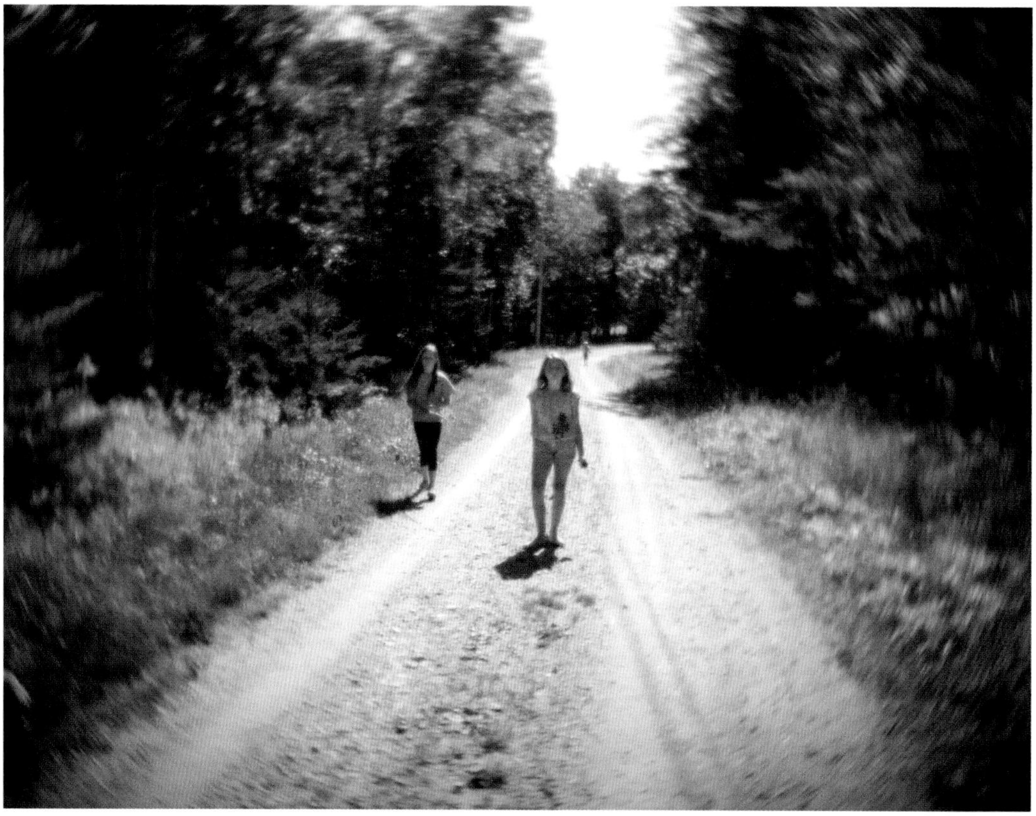

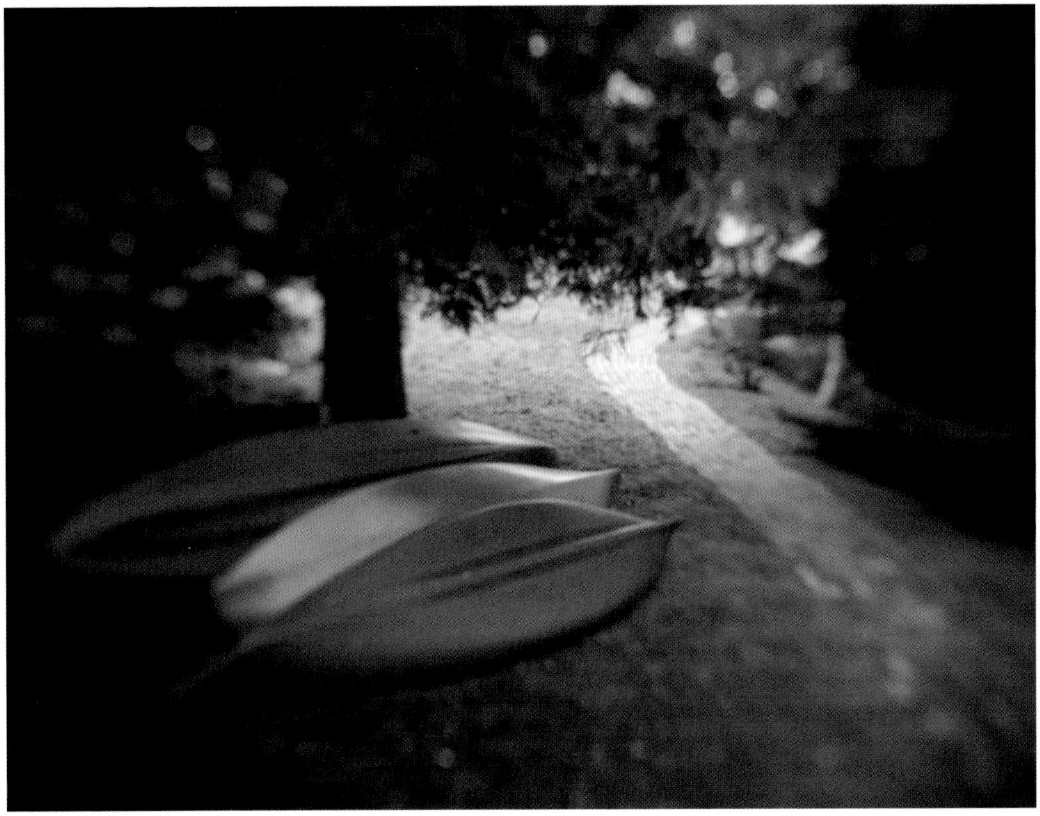

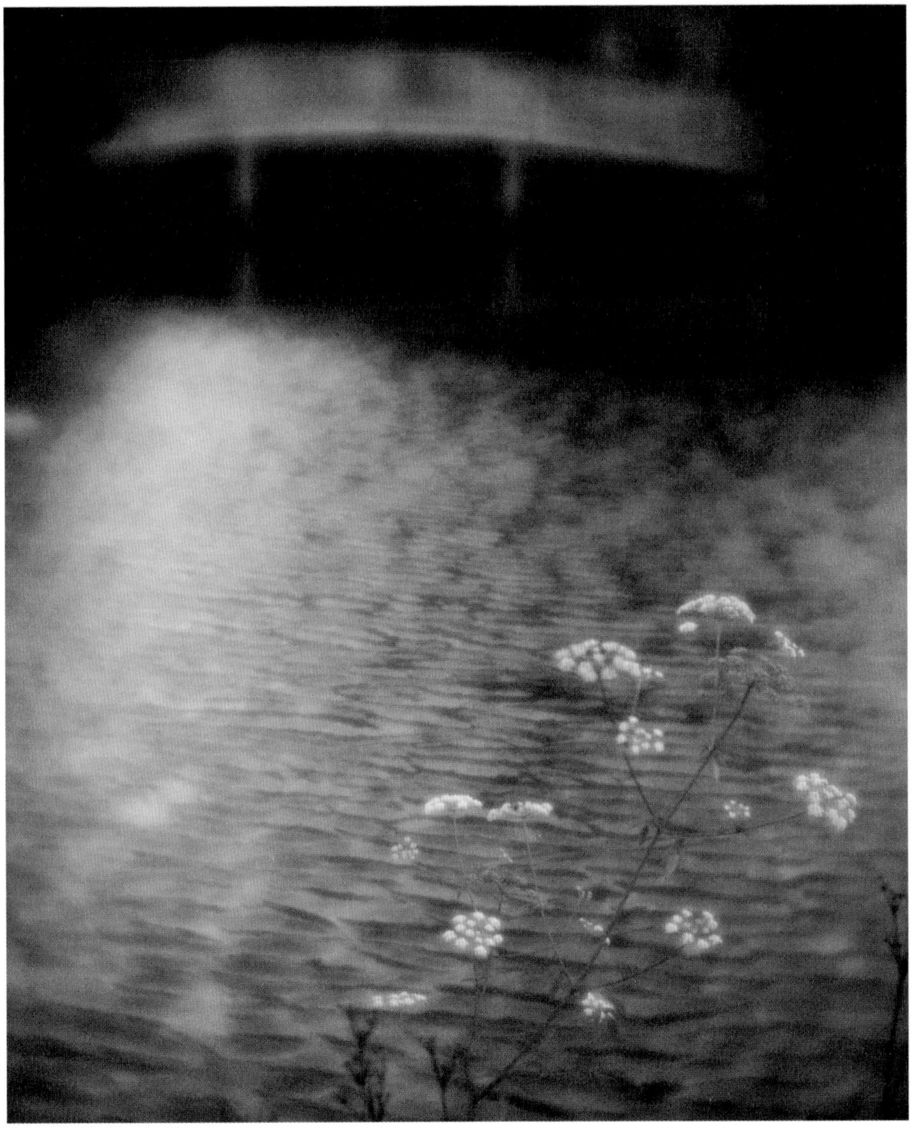

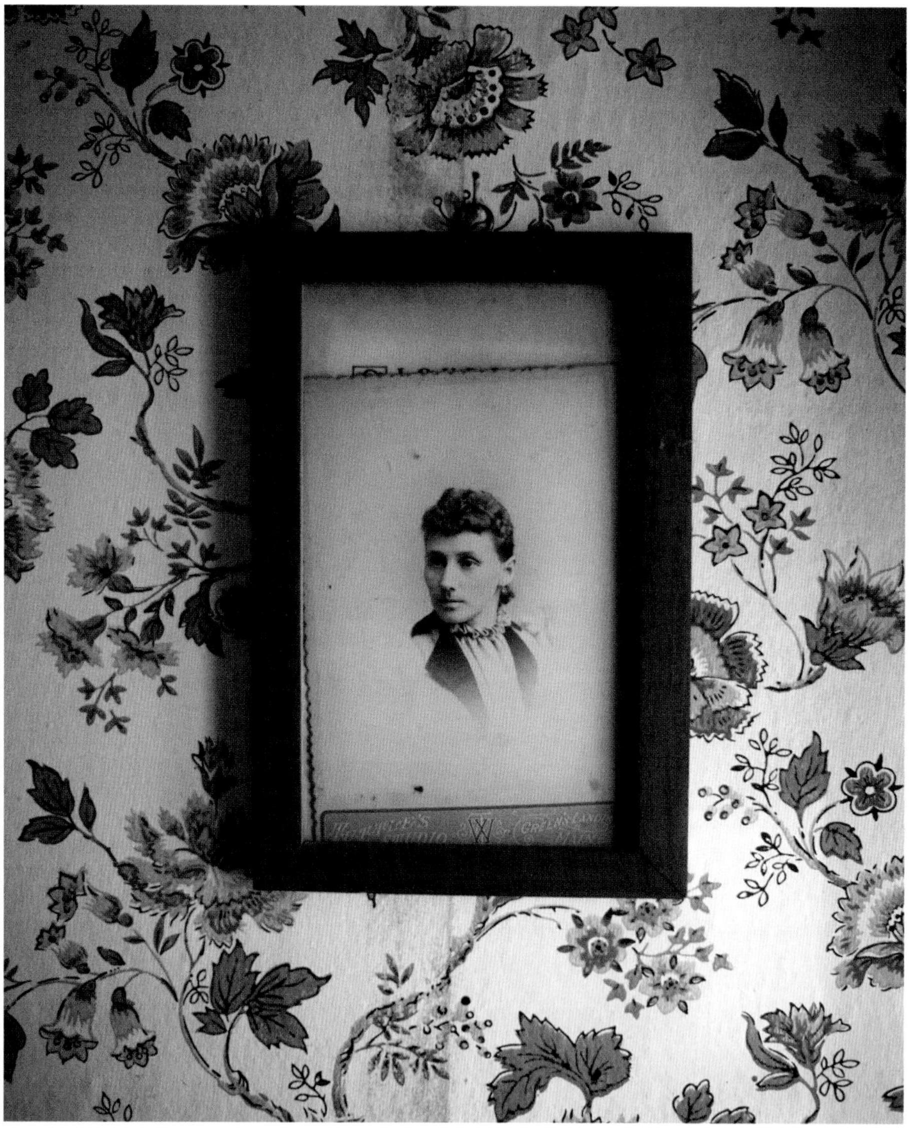

Presence

I never knew you,
yet I feel you in
each room that is
a hallowed space,
unchanging and
remembered.
Sacred.

I hear you,
whispering
through the wallpaper
that is frayed
and steeped
in melancholy
at your leaving.

I see you,
leaning in, listening
to the ladies laughter.
Your quick hands
make light work.
Small renovations,
of disorderly lives.

snip snip

I look where you looked,
past the bird house
and the tree and
I wonder
at your presence
in my heart.

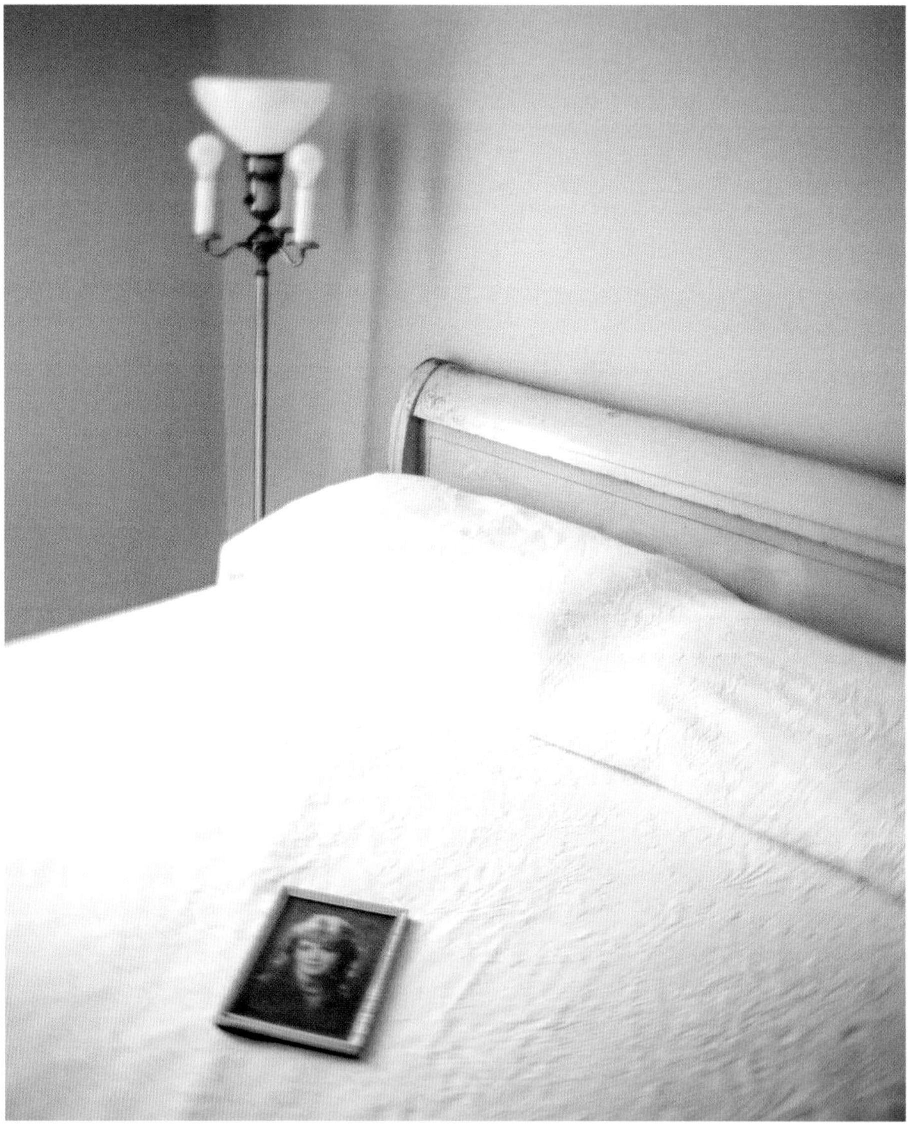

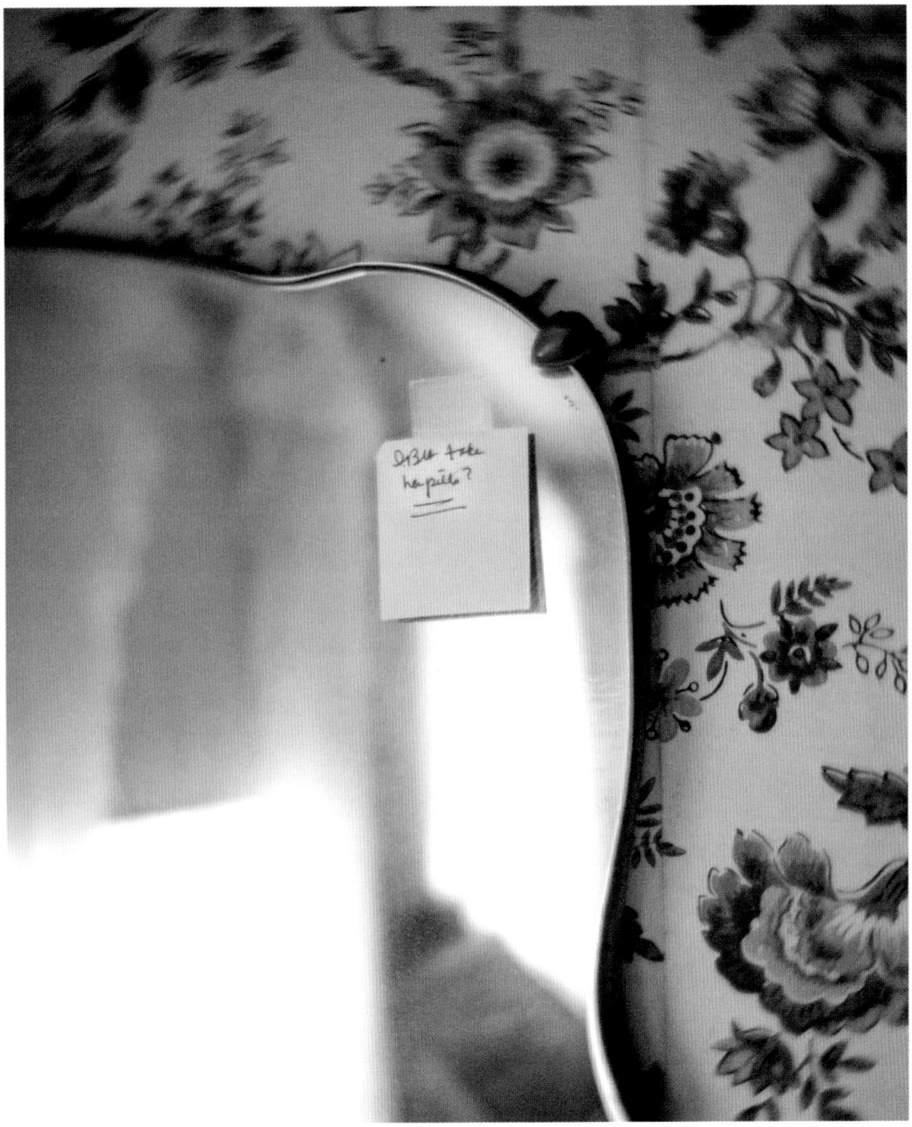

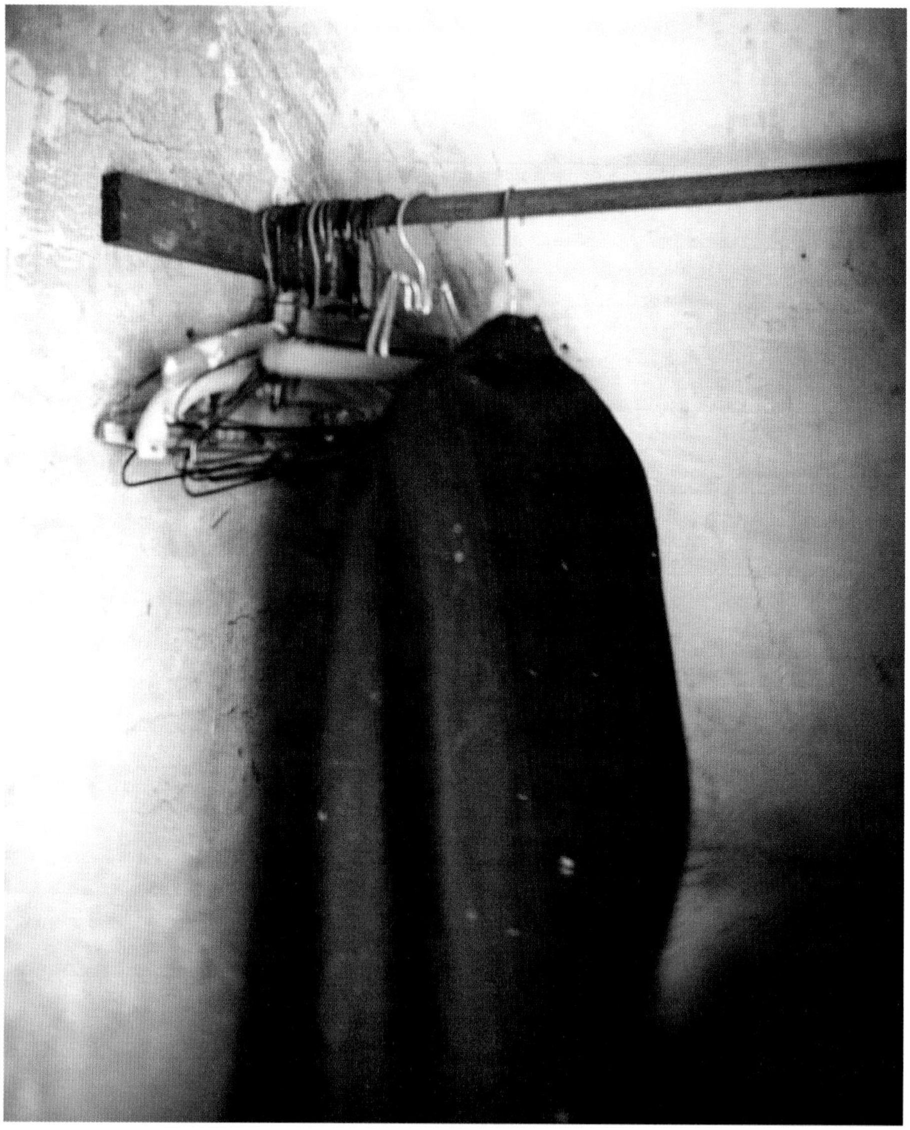

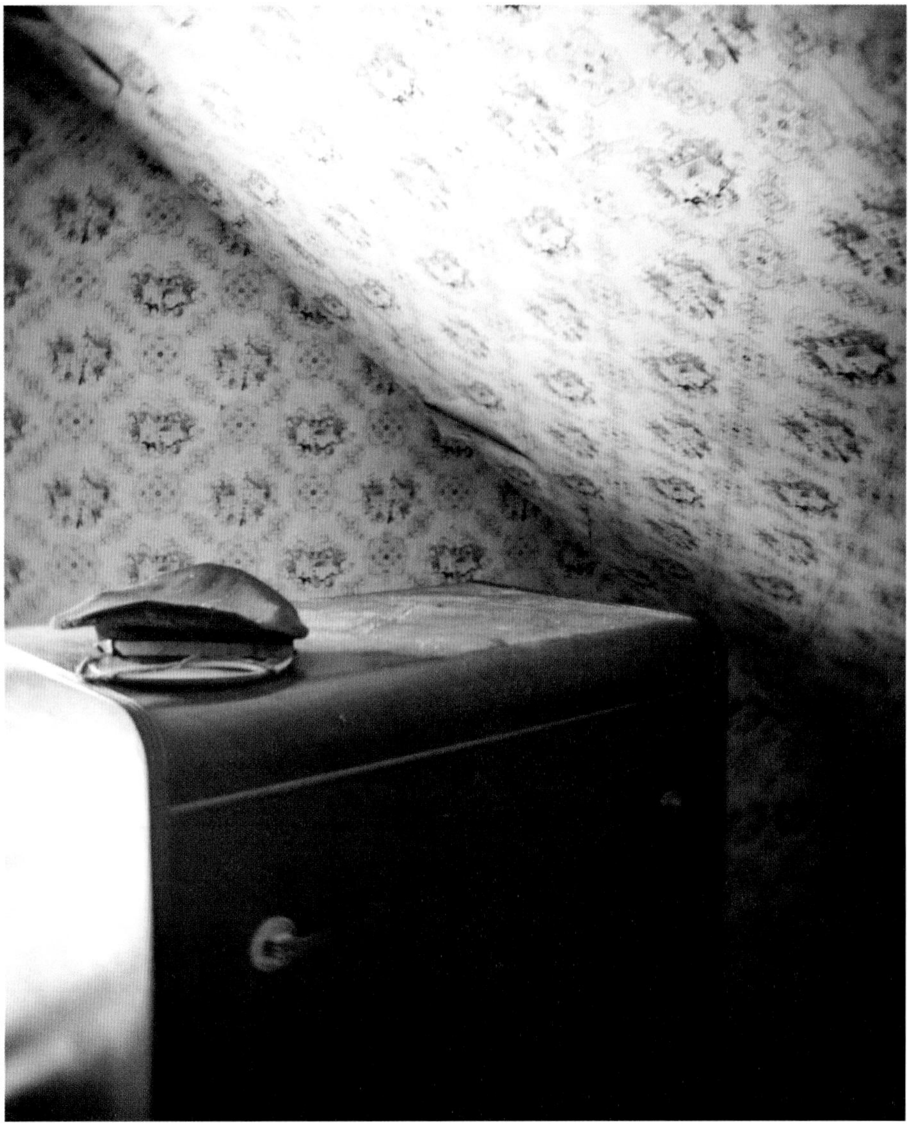

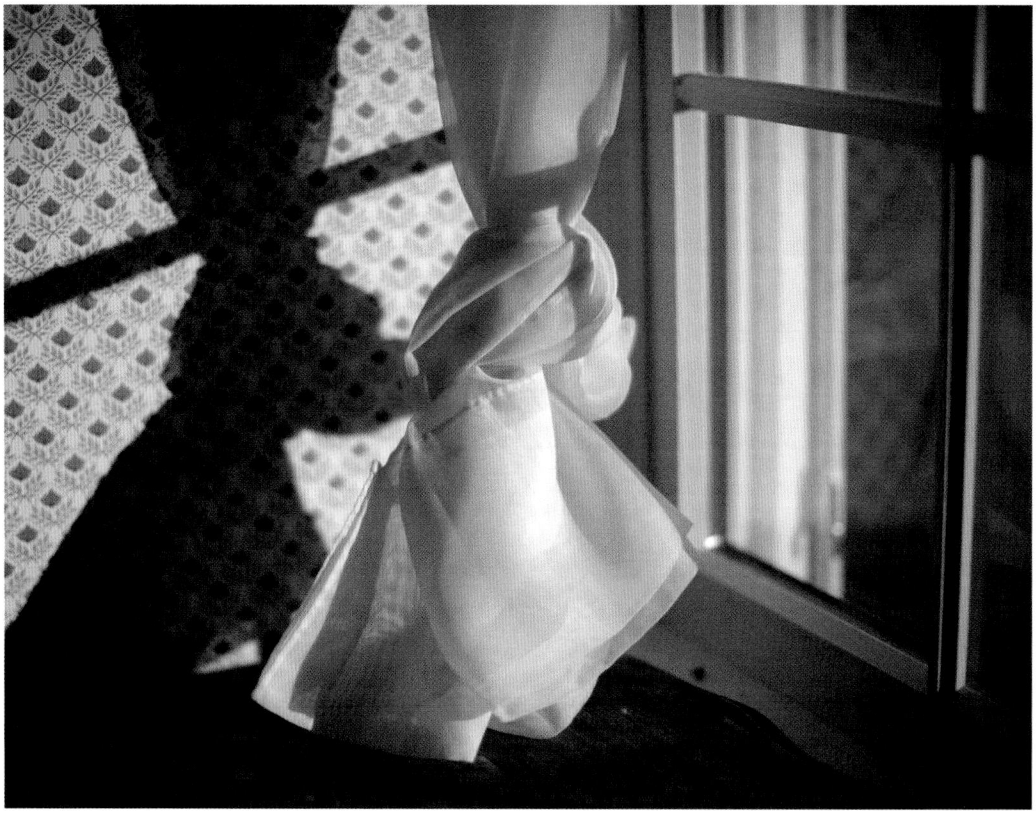

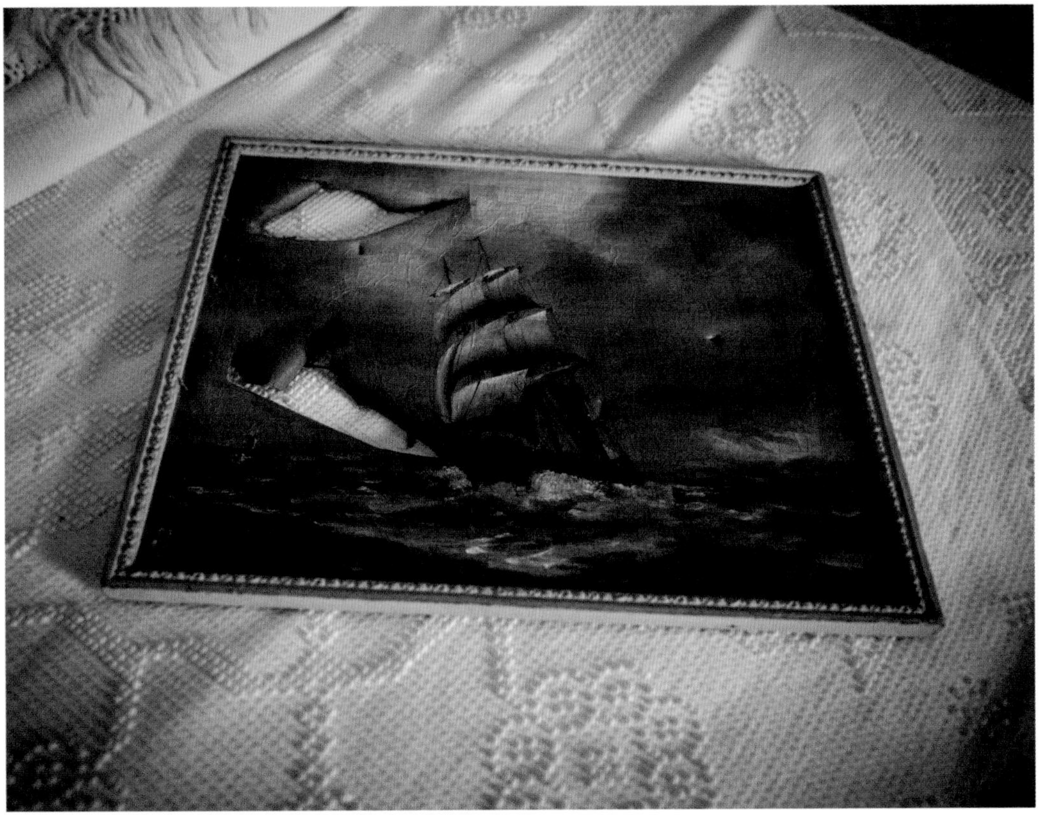

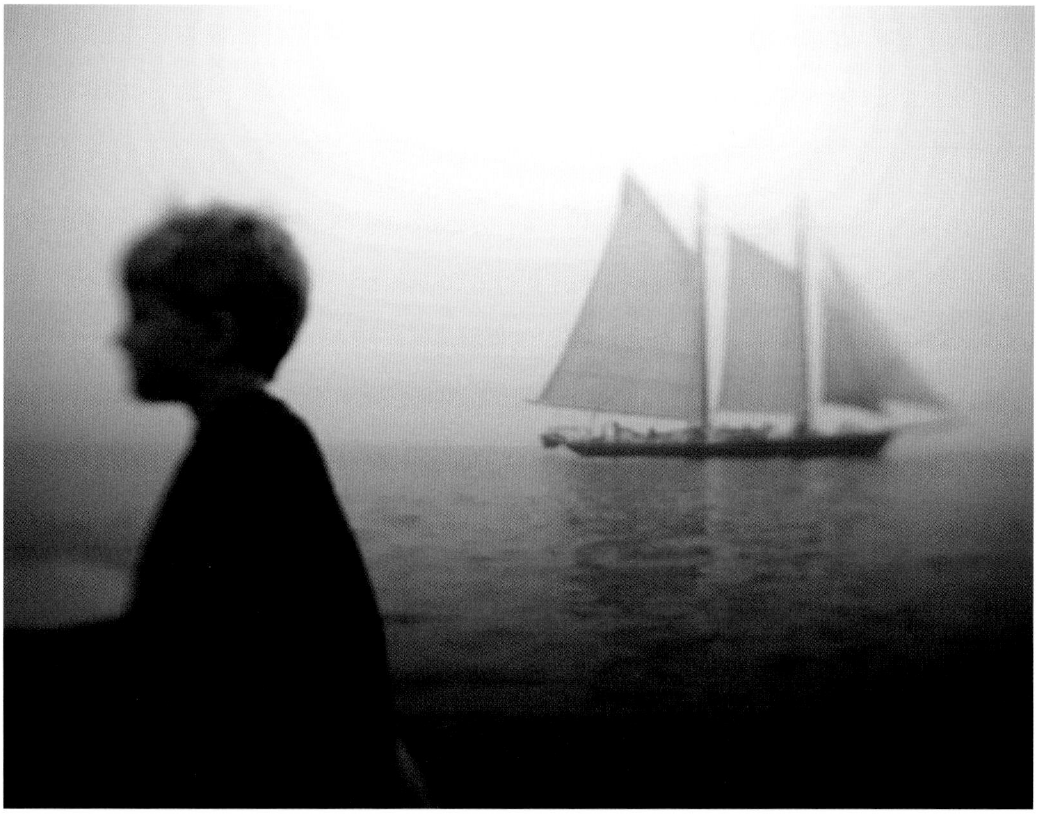

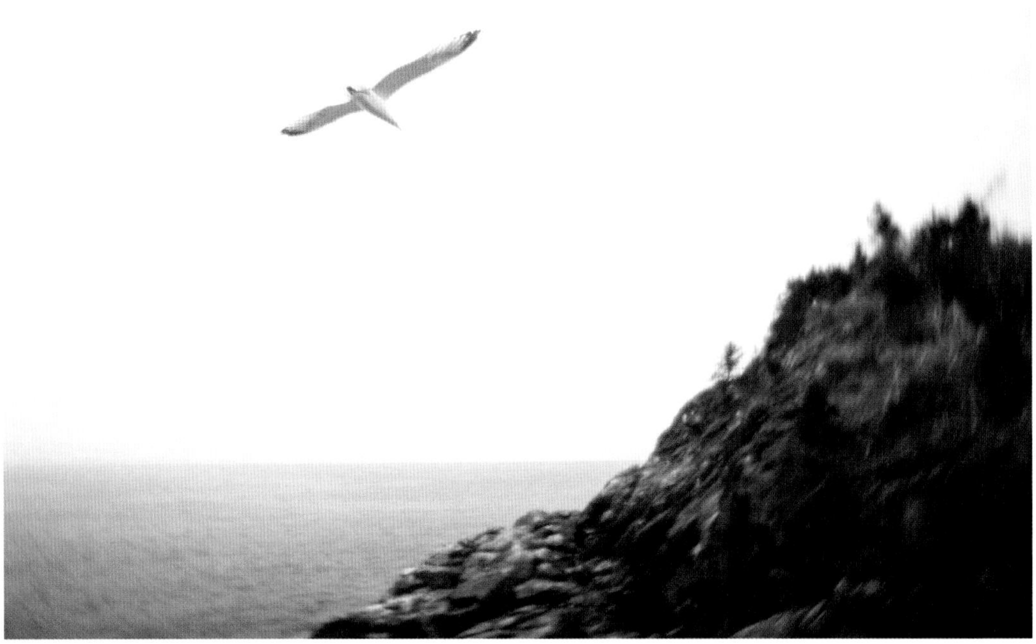

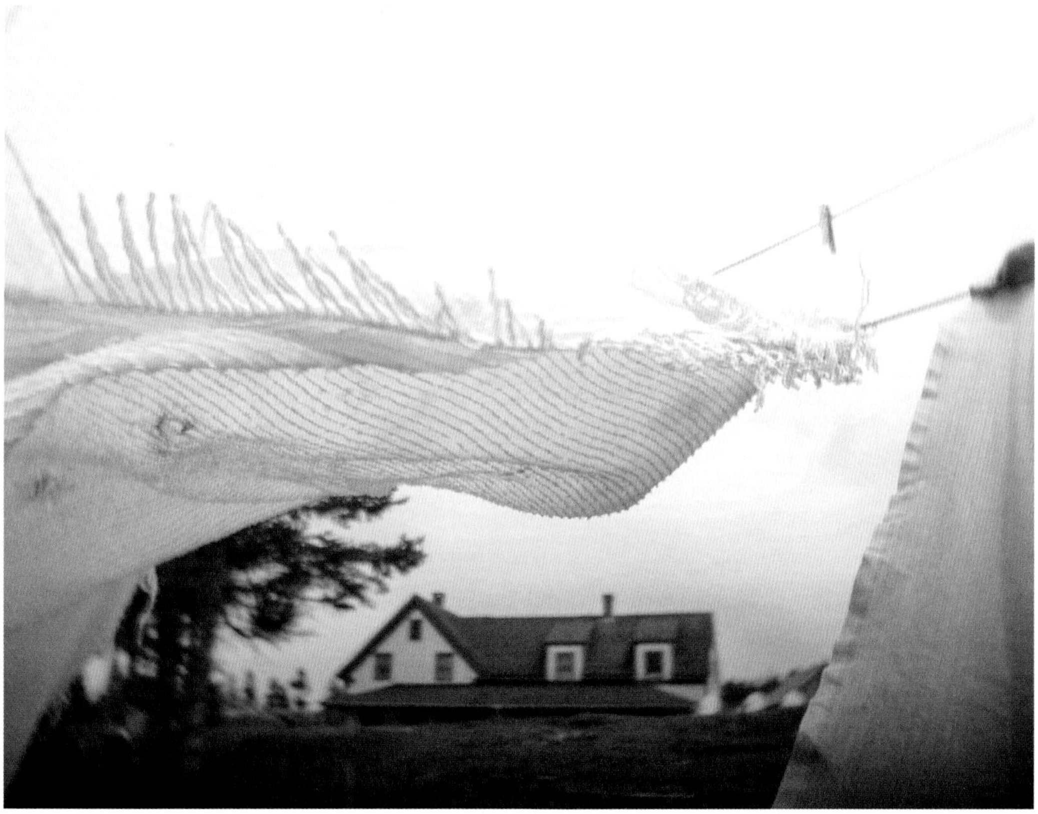

Benevolence

Amidst the crumbling
of the old foundation,
a lone foxglove
waves tenderly.

The roses, once so bold,
are now forgotten
stumps of stringy growth
untended.

Benevolent still,
the lone apple tree
stands upon the hill.
Her boughs curl and arch
against the sea,
resisting, time
itself.

Fruit falls
nourishing the soil.
Testament,
to absence.

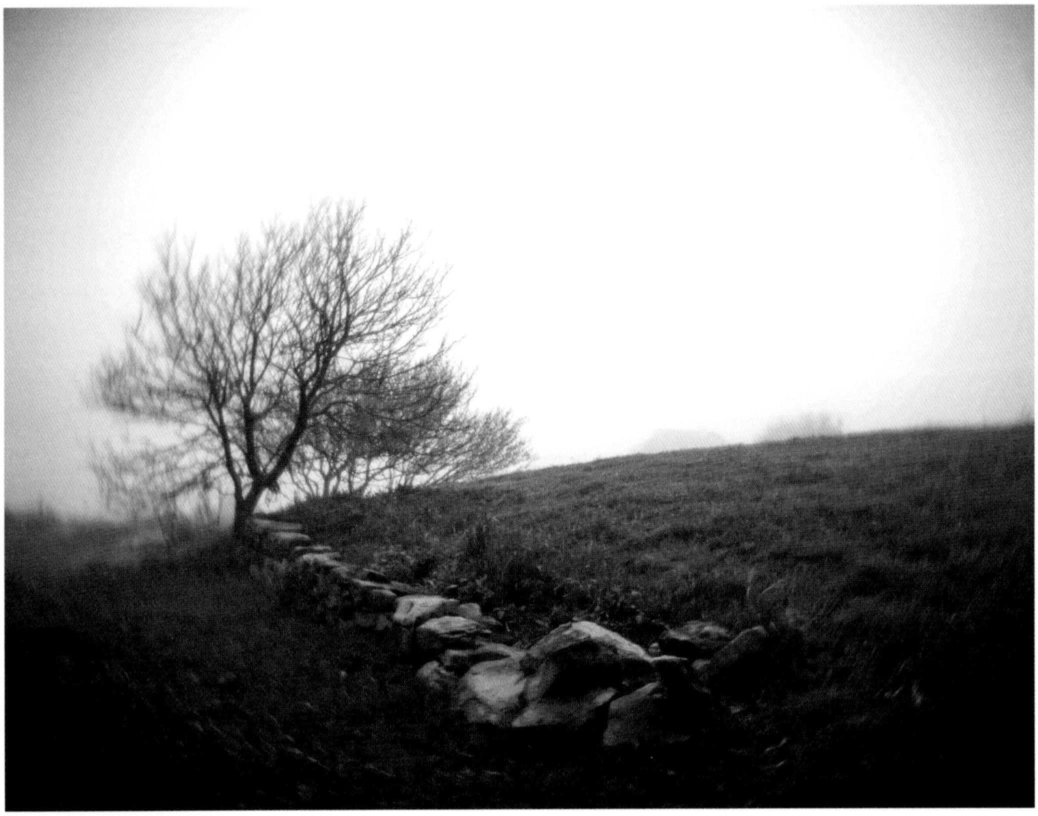

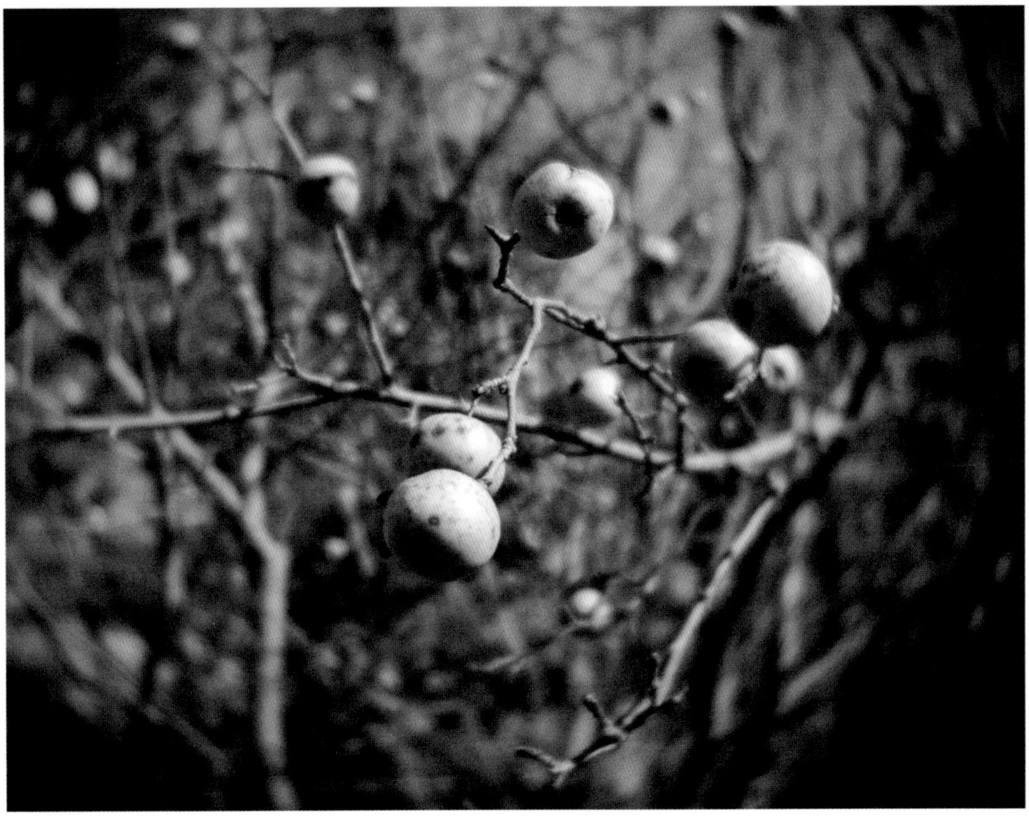

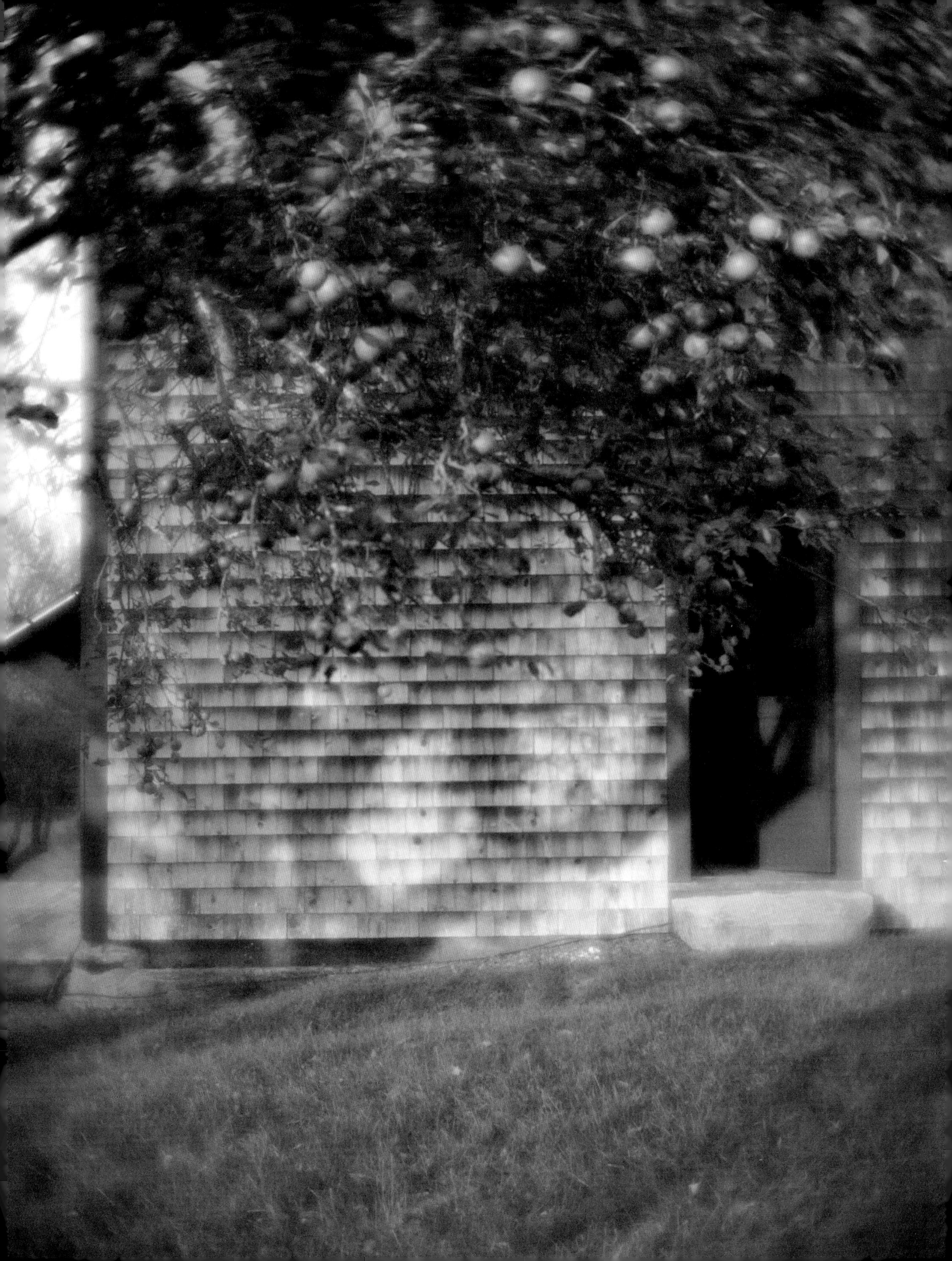

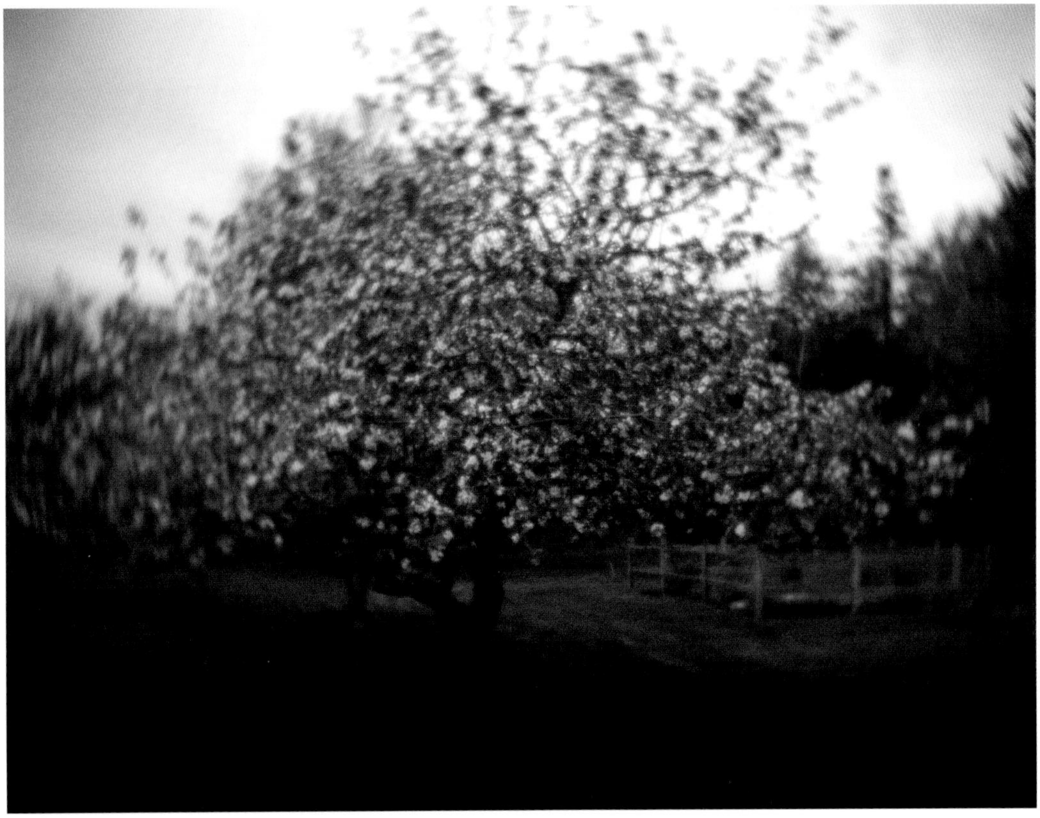

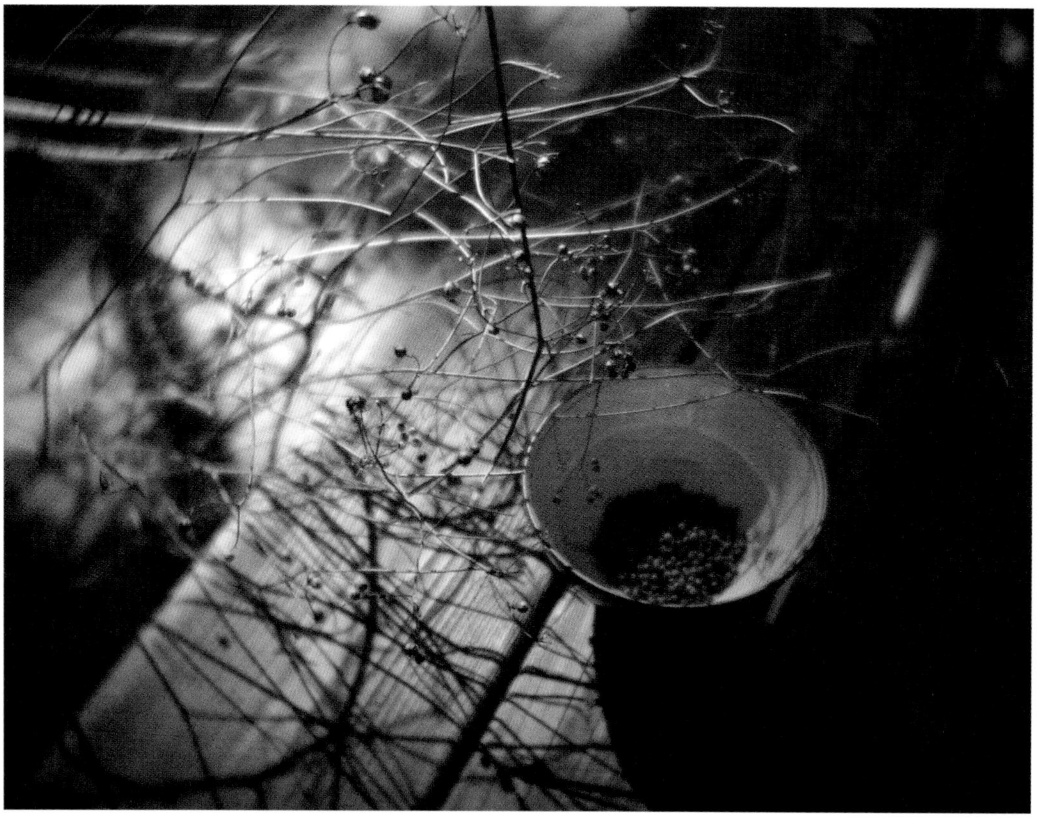

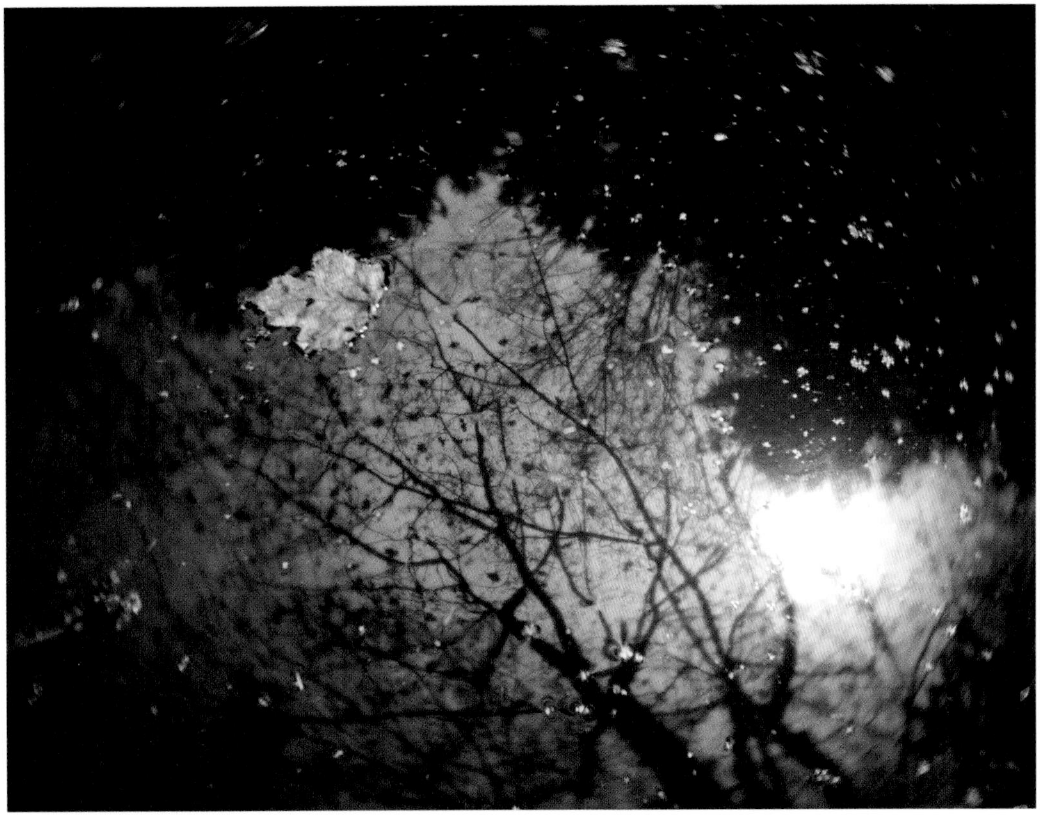

Plates

Afterword

Sal Taylor Kydd

There are over 4,000 islands off the coast of Maine, from small rocky outcroppings to thriving islands with vibrant communities of fishermen, artists and summer visitors. I have been coming to one of these, Deer Isle, for the last twenty years, as our family has made our annual pilgrimage, crossing the bridge and driving over the causeway, returning to the home of my husband's ancestors to share in some of its beauty and heritage. This place has become a touchstone for our family, grounding us in a shared identity, a place we have the privilege of returning to, summer after summer, year after year.

With time I have come to explore many of the other islands of the Penobscot Bay from Vinalhaven, to Matinicus, from Deer Isle to Monhegan, visiting in the bustling months of summer, but also in the offseason, when the visitors have left and "stillness settles;" when only those truly committed to this somewhat isolated life remain. Through these years I have relished the opportunity to spend my days more simply and to see my children, when they were young, unwinding the taught strings upon which they balance their busy lives, living in the present, when the fog lingers and the afternoons stretch long.

I am not a native Mainer, I moved to the U.S. many years ago to follow in my father's footsteps; he had also found a home here. I appreciate that I am still a visitor, someone "from away," as the saying goes. But I have discovered a deep connection to these lands of "porcelain, silk, and old silver glinting." It is a connection rooted in a deep appreciation for what it took to endure on these rocky knolls and what it takes to thrive here still. It is a recognition of the tenacity found in this history that draws me to the stories of past generations who crossed the seas to make new lives for themselves. Theirs are the stories I listen for, whispering in the wallpaper, sighing in the leaves, reaching for me, through the ages, in the fog.

Acknowledgments

Every book takes more than one person to bring it together, and I am so very grateful for the support of those that have enabled me on this journey. To Richard Blanco for your insights on my writing. Elizabeth Avedon for your feedback and insight on the design. Elin Spring and Kat Kiernan for your luminous writing. And to Kirsten Surbey, Colin Page, and Allison Worden, for your friendship and ongoing support of my work.

During the course of working on this book I lost two members of my immediate family. The first was my birth father, a man to whom I owe much of what defines me as an artist. Through themes of family history and memory, I've always been working to understand where I come from. How I express these themes in my words and my work draws upon a creative lineage from him, himself a writer, and from those who came before. The second loss was of my brother Simon. Simon was the first person to really introduce me to the art world, he was the one I would go to exhibitions with, talking and looking at the work, drawing connections, understanding its relevance to me and my world. Both of these left me with gifts I will carry with me forever and I will always be so very grateful, whilst forever feeling the hole that their absence leaves in my life.

I'd also like to thank my children Oliver and Lola, who constantly challenge me to do better and to model the life I wish for them. A brave and bold life, one that embraces the world with curiosity, empathy, and openness. And to my husband Steven, my partner in all things, I thank you and I love you.